CONTRASTING STYLES OF INDUSTRIAL REFORM

CONTRASTING STYLES OF INDUSTRIAL REFORM

China and India in the 1980s

George Rosen

THE UNIVERSITY OF CHICAGO PRESS

Chicago and London

GEORGE ROSEN, emeritus professor of economics
at the University of Illinois at Chicago, is book review editor
for the journal *Economic Development
and Cultural Change.*

The University of Chicago Press, Chicago 60637
The University of Chicago Press, Ltd., London

© 1992 by The University of Chicago
All rights reserved. Published 1992
Printed in the United States of America

01 00 99 98 97 96 95 94 93 92   5 4 3 2 1

ISBN (cloth): 0-226-72646-0

Library of Congress Cataloging-in-Publication Data

Rosen, George, 1920–
    Contrasting syles of industrial reform : China and India in the
1980s / George Rosen.
        p.   cm.
    Includes bibliographical references and index.
    1. Industry and state—China.   2. Industry and state—India.
3. China—Economic policy—1976-   4. India—Economic policy—1980–
I. Title.
HD3616.C63R67   1992
338.951′009′048—dc20   91-31762

To the memory of

ALEX ECKSTEIN

AND

PAUL ROSENSTEIN-RODAN

good friends and pioneers in American

studies of the

Chinese and Indian economies

CONTENTS

PREFACE

This book, contrasting economic reform styles in China and India, brings my research career to a full circle. My first professional research, embodied in my Ph.D. thesis, sought to examine the longer-run implications for the United States of the industrialization of China and India. It was undertaken at the suggestion and under the guidance of Frank D. Graham of Princeton in the late 1940s, and it was this work that brought me into the field of economic development. It is both fitting, and another one of the coincidences of my career, that my final research in an academic position undertaken before my retirement returns to the China-India theme.

My 1949 dissertation was completed without my having set foot in either India or China. Since then I have lived and worked for extended periods in both countries, and this book reflects my research in both since 1983. China was largely closed to visits by American scholars from 1949 to the late 1970s. However I tried to keep up with the literature on economic development in that country. I was also a good friend of Alex Eckstein, with whom I would discuss those developments when we met. In the 1950s and 1960s I spent almost four years in India, working as an economist with the Massachusetts Institute of Technology Center for International Studies and the Ford Foundation. Max Millikan, the Center's director at the time, Wilfred Malenbaum and Paul Rosenstein-Rodan, the two directors of the Center's India project during my work there, all had strong interests in both India's and China's economic development. Malenbaum wrote explicitly on comparisons of the two countries, most recently in 1990, while Rosenstein-Rodan's interest in India's development went back to the 1930s at the University of London, where some of India's future leading economists and intellectuals were his students and friends. During my four years of work in India I met many of India's leading economists not only as professional colleagues, but as

friends, and it is this friendship and collegiality that made my experience of and in India such a satisfying one.

My first visit to China took place in 1984. I had returned to India
in 1983 for a year at the University of Hyderabad to explore various
economic changes between my earlier research of the 1960s and the
1980s. On my departure from India I was able to visit Jilin University
of Technology in Changchun for six weeks, as a result of an exchange
program between the university and the University of Illinois at
Chicago. While I do not know Chinese, I found that visit so interesting and unusual that for the first time in my career I kept a daily
journal.

That short visit whetted my appetite for a longer stay. That opportunity came in 1986, when I was invited by William Speidel, the director of the Johns Hopkins–Nanjing University Center for Chinese
and American Studies, to serve as one of the American faculty at that
Center in its first year, 1986–87. My wife, Sylvia Vatuk, and I lived
and worked at the Nanjing Center, and over that period of time became friends with Chinese faculty and staff, with Chinese students at
the Center, and with other Chinese in Nanjing as well as with American faculty and staff and students. From exchange of ideas with those
friends and associates, and from visits to Chinese factories and other
institutions, I was able to gain some of the perspectives on the
Chinese reform process that I develop in this book. That stay too
stimulated the idea of examining some of the contrasts in the reform
process between China and India, and made me feel that I could do
this even though I did not know Chinese.

In the winter of 1987–88 I spent four months in India examining
the effects of Rajiv Gandhi's economic reforms upon Indian industry.
An American Institute of Indian Studies research grant made it possible for me to visit various Indian cities to talk to friends, economists,
businessmen, and officials on the subject of those reforms and their
effects. That extended visit was very fruitful professionally, but, more
than that, it turned out to be one of the most enjoyable experiences of
my life. Visiting friends, many of whom I had not seen for twenty
years, and places I had not seen for as long a period, was a homecom-
ing. The warmth of that experience remains unforgettable. This was
reinforced by another visit to India in the winter of 1989, when I accompanied my wife on her research in Madras and Hyderabad. During that time I worked at the Madras Institute of Development
Studies and again at Hyderabad University. Between that last visit to
India and the appearance of this book, Sukhamoy Chakravarty, one of
my oldest friends in India and an economist of great idealism and

courage, died at a relatively early age. His death is a great loss for India and for those who knew him.

In the summer of 1989 I again accompanied my wife, who was doing research in London. I was able to take advantage of that visit to work in the libraries of the School of Asian and African Studies and the London School of Economics to update my knowledge of China and India and, more important, to talk to economists in London and Oxford who were working on the Chinese economy and to benefit from their work.

In the winter of 1989–90 a Woodrow Wilson International Center Fellowship enabled me to write a draft of this book. The Woodrow Wilson Center, whose Asia program is directed by Mary B. Bullock, is an ideal place to carry on research, not only in terms of providing facilities for research and exchange of ideas with fellows and staff, but also in providing access to the wealth of resources at the Library of Congress, to government agencies and embassies, and to numerous scholars and staff of institutions in the Washington area doing research on India and China. The comments on my seminar paper by Paul Kreisberg and Christine Wallich were very useful for my further work. My research assistant at the Wilson Center, Todd Brighton, provided help well beyond the ordinary call of duty, in his efforts to teach me to use a word processor. Prasenjit Duara, who was a fellow at the Center at the same time, was most helpful. Finally both my wife and I have numerous personal friends living and working in and near Washington. They made our stay there an extremely pleasant one, as well as one much too short. While in Washington, too, I was able to present seminars on my work at the University of Maryland, thanks to John Adams, and at the University of Virginia, thanks to John Echeverri-Gent.

My special thanks go to my research assistant at the University of Illinois at Chicago, Buu Ruizhi, for his valuable insights into the Chinese reform process as shown in numerous comments on my earlier drafts. I would also like to thank other Chinese graduate students in the economics department who attended my seminars on the subject and commented on various aspects of it. These include Li Xiao Bo, Lin Zhiyong, Ma Yunxia, Yu Hanying, and Zhang Rhenze. Needless to say, none of them has any responsibility for the opinions expressed in this book, but their presence and their kindness gave me at least some better sense of what I, as a foreigner ignorant of the Chinese language, was writing about.

I list separately the numerous people in India, Nanjing, London, Washington, and Chicago who were so helpful in my writing of this book. I will not give names of Chinese friends in Nanjing on the chance that, for whatever reason, it might be harmful to them in the future, although I see no reason why it should be in terms of what I have written.

I have also benefited by being able to use previously unpublished papers by Lew Fickett, Athar Hussain, T. Manohoran, Peter Mayer, and Jean Oi, and I appreciate their giving me access to those papers. Lina Fruzetti and Akos Ostor provided assistance at a strategic moment, and this contributed significantly to the book's publication.

I would also like to thank M. J. Dutta, director of the American Committee for Asian Economic Studies, who gave me an opportunity to present a summary of my ideas in a paper, "India and China: Contrasting Styles of Economic Reform," and orally at a conference in New York City in June 1989; and Gregory Chow, Gary Jefferson, and T. N. Srinivasan for their comments on that paper, as well as other members of the audience who commented on my presentation. (This paper was subsequently published in the *Journal of Asian Economics* vol. 1, no. 2 [Fall 1990]).

Warm thanks are also due to Kusum Nair, who arranged and chaired a seminar based on my India-China work at the University of Wisconsin South Asia Conference in Madison on November 3, 1990. Edward Friedman, Walter (Terry) Neale, Wayne Nafziger, and Jin Wang made very helpful comments on that paper itself, as well as suggestions for longer treatment of the topic, and Wayne later commented on a draft of the book. I also benefited from their own work on topics related to the subject, and Ed Friedman introduced me to Jay Taylor's ambitious book contrasting the two societies, *The Dragon and the Wild Goose: China and India* (New York, 1987). I completed writing the text of the book in early 1991, before the Indian elections in June of that year.

I also had the opportunity to give seminars on my work in the economics department of the University of Illinois at Chicago, and I thank the members of the department who participated. The support of Barry Chiswick, department head, and Lynn Lacey, administrative officer, was most helpful to my work, as was that of deans Ralph Westfall, Marcus Alexis, and Robert Abrams.

This book would not have been possible without the very great effort of Yvonne Marshall, who typed numerous drafts of the manuscript, and of Dianne Scruggs, who typed the final draft. And its appearance reflects the interest, confidence, and work of Geoffrey Huck, economics editor of the University of Chicago Press, whose support and friendship made the final product what you see. The manuscript has been substantially improved by the editorial review and suggestions of Carol Saller, all of which made the final version of the book easier to read and to understand. Finally it would not have been carried out without the close collaboration of my wife, Sylvia Vatuk. I can honestly say that we are both responsible for whatever merits the text has; I alone am responsible for its defects.

Contributors, not previously named, whose support in one way or another made this book possible in its final form, are: in India, at the American Institute of Indian Studies, Pradeep Mehinderatta, L. S. Suri, and P. V. Rao; in Delhi, I. J. Ahluwalia, L. Chakravarty, I. Dalmia, P. N. Dhar, and P. Tandon; in Bombay, R. S. Bhatt, S. A. Dave, S. K. Gupta, F. Mehta, C. Rangarajan, J. Sabavala, S. Sabavala, and J. C. Sandesara; in Hyderabad, J. Bjorkman, G. Gouri, H. Mazumdar, R. Radhakrishna, J. M. Reddy, S. Sarupria, and V. V. N. Somayajulu; in Madras, S. Guhan, C. T. Kurien, T. Krishnan, S. Ranade, N. Tyabji, and A. Vaidyanathan; in Bangalore, K. S. Krishnaswamy; in Calcutta, K. Brill, M. Brill, S. N. Chaudhuri, B. Datta, A. Mitra, former state finance minister, A. Mitra, I.C.S., and R. Sau.

In China, at the Nanjing/Hopkins Center, R. Fogarty, K. Kadish, S. Parry, L. Slawecki, and J. Townsend.

In England, J. Enos, S. Epstein, A. Hussain, C. Lin, I. M. D. Little, A. Mayer, H. Myint, and I. G. Patel.

In Washington, D.C., at the Woodrow Wilson Center, T. Barassi, Z. David, E. Doane, M. Poggioli, and S. Reppert. Others in or near Washington: A. D. Barnett, S. J. Burki, J. Carroll, W. Diamond, L. Felsenthal, W. Gilmartin, H. Harding, W. Hauser, N. Islam, J. Lewis, M. Lipton, L. Mansingh, M. Massen, P. Medhora, J. Mellor, P. Muncie, J. Riedel, T. Robinson, T. Timberg, D. Werner, and M. H. You.

Introduction:
The Rationale for the Book

In the world there is only one large Asian country which has conditions similar to China. She went on the capitalist path after independence. Britain and the United States gave her assistance and the
Soviet Union also. International circumstances were favorable for
her, her average farmland per person is much more than in China.
But she remains a developing country. Thee are enormous numbers
of people hungry, there are ceaseless disturbances in innumerable
social problems.

Her national situation is similar to that of China. She went the
capitalist way, we the socialist one. A comparison between them is
unlikely to show any superiority of capitalism over socialism.
CHENG JUNSHENG, "To Persist," *People's Daily*

Despite important differences in the political and social systems
and even in the economic structure [of India and China], there were
sufficient similarities in the problems facing them, such as those
arising from their large size, high demographic pressure, . . . dependence on foreign technology and problems of centralized planning
and regulation of resource allocation to stimulate . . . interest
[among both Indian and Chinese economists in a joint seminar on
the two economies].
A. VAIDYANATHAN, *Economic Development of India and China*

CHINA and India have been carrying out significant reforms in
their industrial policy frameworks over the past decade and
longer. The Chinese reforms antedate the economic policy
changes in Eastern Europe; the Indian reforms are not as sharp as
those in China, but they have characteristics of the reform process in
other democracies or near democracies. Thus an examination of
these reform processes may throw light on efforts in other countries.
Significant similarities in the economic situations of China and India, despite their different political and economic systems, provide
the reason for contrasting the reform processes of these countries in a

1

single volume. Indian policymakers have long been interested in China's economic development prospects and policies; Chinese economists have been less interested in the Indian experience, but there is such interest as we shall note.

What are the similarities that contribute to that interest, apart from the fact that they are neighbors? An obvious one is that they are the two largest countries in the world in terms of population, each having about one billion people, with China somewhat larger. At the start of their development process each had more than two-thirds of its population engaged in agriculture; each, as the major direction of its development policy, sought to expand its industrial sector, so that there would be significant shifts in its structures of output and of employment to higher income sectors. By the end of the 1970s each had markedly expanded its industrial sector and India also its service sector. In China the government service sector had expanded, but not other service areas, in large part because Marxist theory regarded services as unproductive. But in spite of this marked expansion in non-agricultural output and employment, and a growth in agricultural output that equaled or exceeded the growth of population, the proportions of the two populations still dependent on agriculture remained at 60 percent or more, while agriculture's share of the national output of each country fell to 30–40 percent.

In both countries total national outputs had increased significantly since 1950, at rates of growth higher than during the first half of the century and higher than the growth rates of their respective populations. Nevertheless the level of per capita income in each country in 1975–80 was on the order of U.S.$300.00, and both countries were classed with the poorer of the developing countries. In both countries too the problem of providing employment for a labor force growing more rapidly than their populations and with rising expectations of employment was serious. Today both China and India have expectations of a better quality of life in terms of improved health, longevity, education, and freedom from hunger and starvation, all of which were promised results of independence and revolution. Such improvement did occur in both countries, but there are significant differences, reflecting their different approaches to those ends.

There are other similarities of the two economies. Both China and India are very large countries geographically with wide variations among their regions, with the coastal areas tending to have higher levels of development, higher incomes, greater contacts with foreign countries, and higher levels of industry and trade. China is ethnically more homogenous than India, which places less political pressure on the Chinese government to equalize development between the different regions. But both countries have been committed to raising economic levels in the poorer interior regions and to greater equality among regions; in both countries, too, reasons of defense led to siting defense-related industries in interior provinces felt to be less vulnerable to external attacks.

Both India and China, because of their sizes and their positions in Asia, consider themselves to be major political actors in their region, as well as in the world. This implies certain levels of industrial development, an ability to produce inputs for defense industries and military outputs, and a level of technology capable of meeting their needs for modern weapons and defense systems. Both countries have histories of foreign occupation and invasion. India was a British colony for almost two hundred years before independence; China, while not a colony, had been involved in numerous wars and skirmishes with foreign powers invading and attempting to annex or control portions of its territory in the hundred years before the Communist victory. Both, as a result, are strongly nationalist and are sensitive to any felt threat of dependency in relation to foreign countries and economic groups. Their development programs and policies reflect that strong nationalism and fear of dependency.

Finally the new governments of both countries, after achieving independence and successful revolution, adopted programs of industrialization based in part on the methods of the Soviet Union which appeared so successful after the Second World War. These included the development of heavy industry, especially steel, and the capital goods sector, with associated high rates of investment; the deliberate downplaying of consumer goods industries; and the diversion of savings and investment from agriculture to industry. Both countries adopted inward-oriented industrialization policies, in part on grounds of nationalism and/or Marxism, in part on the basis of the depressed history of world trade between the two world wars. They both adopted economic planning and the expansion of the public sector as the instruments for the hoped-for industrial development. But there were major differences in the broader political and economic structures of the two countries that determined the characteristics of the two resulting planning and industrial systems.

After the Communist revolution and victory in China in 1949 a dictatorship was established with all power concentrated in the hands of the Communist party and its leaders. The policies of that leadership were implemented at the regional level by local and provincial party officers and government officials. Within a relatively short time all private enterprises were nationalized; at first former owners were often employed as managers, but by the end of the first decade these had been forced out and replaced by managers controlled by government ministries or party secretaries. Production in the factories was determined by targets set in the central plan; distribution was handled through government agencies at prices set by those agencies. All revenues above costs were forwarded to the central government and all investment was handled through the government budget; workers were assigned to the plant by the labor agency, employment was for life, and changing jobs was not allowed. Wages were determined by seniority and all workers were paid according to the same scale of wages. In the rural sector after an early reform that redistributed land among the peasants in the villages, the private plots were rather quickly eliminated and replaced by a system of communal landownership, with production and work distribution and wages under the control of party officials of the commune. All output above that required for local needs was sold to state distribution agencies at fixed prices, and distributed by state agencies throughout the country. In this revolutionary society no legal framework existed embodying contracts of mutual responsibility and limits to actions by the state with respect to the individual or the enterprise.

A similar centralization of power held true in the political field. All power was concentrated in the party and no open debate or opposition was permitted, although there might be some debate within the party before a decision was made. After Mao achieved power and especially following China's economic recovery in the 1950s, ideology became the dominant factor behind economic policy, with possible variations in emergencies or special cases. In the Great Leap Forward of the late 1950s, in order to prevent a concentration of power and control in Beijing that might dampen local economic initiatives, some administrative delegation of power to the level of the province or locality was introduced. But at this time the delegation of power was purely administrative and the decisions were largely made at the center. Since the central government controlled all funding in its budget, there was no need for a credit-banking system or a macroeconomic control agency, which also had no place in Marxist theory. In the first decade of party rule, before the Great Leap Forward and the subsequent sharp policy swings, the Communist regime achieved major advances in both industrial and agricultural production. Following the Great Leap, despite those policy swings, the average output continued to grow but at a slow rate; there were also significant moves toward greater equality of income, and China was successful in achieving greater literacy of the people, improving health, and raising average life expectancy by a significant amount (if one disregards the effects of famine and the forced dispossession and persecution of "rightist" and other identified opponents) by spreading school and health facilities throughout the country.

The domination of policy by ideology contributed to the sharp swings of policy and achievement that characterized China's economic history in the prereform period. Policies, driven by ideology, were carried to extremes that neglected or underemphasized goals, leading to a later sharp policy shift in favor of a neglected goal. One of these ideologically driven policy swings culminated in the Cultural Revolution, which was a mass revolutionary movement led by Mao Zedong to overturn the leaders of the less ideology-driven wings of the party, who had taken power after the collapse of the Great Leap Forward and introduced other policies that Mao opposed. After a decade of the Cultural Revolution and following the death of Mao, the political and economic results of that movement and of its purges and excesses led directly to the growth-oriented "four modernization" policies and leadership of Deng Xiaoping.

India's newly independent government was revolutionary in replacing foreign rule by Indian rule, establishing a democratic system of government in the place of a more or less benevolent despotism, and introducing a "socialistic pattern of society" in place of a capitalist society. But the new political and economic system retained significant elements of the preindependence system and intellectual framework. The democratic political system was influenced by the British parliamentary system, which many of the new leaders knew from their own education and experience in England. The new economic system was influenced by the Soviet experience but was based far more on the ideas of British Fabian democratic socialism than on orthodox Marxism or its Russian variations. In addition, the wartime economic administration of the British left an administrative mechanism and a trained administrative group that could, and would, be adapted to a war on poverty and underdevelopment following the war against Germany and Japan. The Indian industrial sector at independence was almost entirely private. This was largely retained with some marginal nationalization, but on top of that sector was established a large public sector which owned most, if not all, of "the commanding heights." The infrastructure sectors of communications and transportation had been nationalized before independence; the new power sector was in the public sector. Planning had the support of leading private businessmen as well as of Nehru. A Planning Commission was established but it was apart from the regular government ministries. With Prime Minister Nehru's great interest in economic development and planning, the commission had a great deal of influence. Under his successors that influence diminished markedly relative to that of the regular ministries, especially the Finance Ministry (which prepared the budget), the prime minister's secretariat, the various state chief ministers, and other political figures insofar as the plans affected their states. The British left a central banking system, the Reserve Bank of India (RBI) and a system of macroeconomic policy control; the largest private bank, the State Bank of India, was nationalized soon after independence.

In the agricultural sector there was a land reform soon after independence, which redistributed some of the land of the largest landowners, especially that of the local potentates who had supported the British. In effect land was distributed to the peasants who had previously cultivated but not owned the land, or was divided among family members of larger landowning farmers. A class of bullock capitalists, owning plots of 2.5 to 15 acres, became the largest group among the landowning households, owning half the total land, but over a quarter of the peasants were landless, while the large landowners with holdings of 15 acres or more still owned almost 40 percent of the land.[1] Private ownership in land was never replaced by another system.

Finally India, shortly after independence, prepared and adopted a constitution that laid out the rights of the individual versus the state and that defined and allocated the powers of government between the central and state governments, giving the center major economic powers vis-à-vis industry, but giving the states major powers over agriculture and energy distribution; it also allocated taxation powers between the central and state governments, which were given the power to levy excise taxes on manufactured products, and set up a system for the allocation of some central government revenues to the states. India has a legal system that includes a law of contracts, and an independent court system to which citizens can bring cases against each other and against the state. There is freedom of speech and of the press, and a vigorous critical press in Hindi, the regional languages, and English. There is a wide distribution of television sets and radios; while the government runs the radio and television system, it is expected to be nonpartisan in its presentation of news and political events. While the Congress party under the leadership of Nehru and his descendants has been the governing party for almost all the years since independence, there are opposition parties that are critical of its policies; some of the opposition parties have ruled in particular states for many years, and coalitions of opposition parties have won national elections first in 1977 and again in 1989.

There has been a broad continuity in India's economic policy framework since the mid-1950s. Ideologically there has been a broad consensus on some variation of democratic socialism, but the ideology is compatible with a wide range of policy options in practice. Indian socialism has been compatible with a large private industrial sector, but that sector has functioned under an elaborate system of regulations and controls. These controls seek to insure that larger private enterprises conform to the plans or other government economic policies, that they do not waste scarce capital and foreign exchange resources, that they do not behave in a monopolistic fashion, and that they provide appropriate working conditions and welfare provisions for their workers. The nominally independent public-sector enterprises operate under the same controls, but are also overseen directly by appropriate ministries and other government agencies, and by Parliament. The central government set up a network of development banks to provide finance for private enterprise for approved expansions; the various state governments also set up their own industrial finance corporations to provide funding for larger firms, as well as for small-scale enterprises within their state boundaries. The small-scale industrial sector was both assisted by various concessions and programs and protected from competition from larger firms. Through the RBI and government ownership of all commercial banks, the central government effectively controlled the supply of money and bank credit for the entire economy. There is free mobility of labor within India both among jobs and between country and city.

This system works reasonably effectively in establishing a broad industrial base for the country, and in building certain high-tech, often defense-related, installations. But the rate of industrial growth slackened in the later 1960s and 1970s: there were major inefficiencies in the use of scarce resources, India was lagging in new areas of industrial technology, costs of production were high, and neither the quality nor the variety of goods produced by Indian manufacturers were of world standards. This was in spite of the fact that India has one of the largest pools of skilled professional scientists and technical workers in the world. These problems were not of the high drama of the Cultural Revolution that in effect forced reforms in China, but they were sufficiently important to India to persuade Indira Gandhi and her son to initiate an industrial reform process.

Thus India and China began their reforms for similar reasons. While both had achieved major industrial advances since they began their ambitious programs of economic development in the 1950s, in both there had been a slowing down of those growth rates in comparison with both past achievements and projected goals. This slowdown was combined with apparent massive inefficiencies in the use of resources and with the waste of scarce resources. Industrial growth had not achieved some of the broader development goals of the two countries in terms of improved standards of living and greater availability of consumer goods for the bulk of their populations, and this lag threatened internal popular support for both governments. In addition the leaders of both countries recognized that their industries were lagging technologically in the face of the rapid advances occurring elsewhere, and that this threatened the political leadership roles envisioned by those leaders for their countries in the world and in the region. Thus for both internal and external political reasons the leaders of China and India recognized the need for accelerating industrialization in order both to raise their rates of overall economic growth and to speed the overall restructuring of their economies, so that incomes would rise more rapidly and in the process benefit larger proportions of the two populations than in the past. They also sought both to raise the quality of their industrial outputs and adopt advanced technologies in production. In both countries too, the year 2000 was set as an interim target for achieving some of those goals. To achieve these goals both countries introduced reforms in the functioning of their economic systems.

The purpose of this book is to examine the reform processes and results in China and India in the decade of the 1980s. Their economic performances in terms of goals, achievements, and problems are of interest not only to their own inhabitants, but to the world at large. They contain over one-third of the world's total population. Their economic futures are of importance to anyone interested in the world's future on grounds both of broad humanitarian interest and of narrower self-interest. Their industrial successes and failures can have significant political impact with respect to peace in Asia and the world, and on the economic structures and trade patterns of all countries of the world, including the United States. Their experiences too may throw light on the processes and problems of economic policy change and reform in other countries, developed or developing.

This book is not an attempt to compare the economic growth rates or income distribution of India and China since the reform period began. That is a very complex job that requires putting the economic statistics of the two countries on a comparable basis. Subramanian Swamy has attempted just such a comparison for a period from 1950 through the early periods of reform to the mid- or late 1980s, placing this too in a broader historical perspective. It is a unique and important work, and I will refer to it when relevant to my own; but it is not my focus of interest.[2] Rather what I am attempting is a comparison of the processes of economic reform in the two countries, or, in other words, of the political economy of the economic reforms. Economic reform is a political process. The leadership of the governing party must decide that change in economic policy is desirable; it must determine the directions of change and decide what policies should be emphasized and in what sequence; it must then persuade the wider party and public to approve those desired changes; and it must implement the approved changes through the appropriate agencies of the government. These are largely political decisions and the process is therefore a political one, even though the reforms themselves may have narrow economic ends.

I intend to set the industrial reforms within the framework of the political economies of each country, that is, to examine the relationship of the economic reforms to the policy-making system of each country. There is the obvious difference between the two systems that China is a dictatorship of the Communist party, while India is a democracy, although one party has been in power at the center for most of the forty-five years since India became independent in 1947. (That party, the Congress party, was defeated in the 1989 national elections). Clearly this basic political difference would effect the economic policy-making process.

In China decision making takes place through the Communist party. Nonparty groups have influence only if they can affect the thinking of the party leaders. In India, with its periodic state and national elections, the governing party and its competitors must be regularly aware of the desires of demand groups that may gain or lose by economic decisions, and whose votes are affected thereby. Such groups may present their desires through members of the governing party, or opposition parties, or through the press, or by actions of one type or another—strikes, fasts, demonstrations. Apart from narrower demand groups, enough of the voting public must be satisfied to give a party or a coalition an electoral majority.

In both countries ideology is an important element in economic policy-making. At one time in China it was seen to govern policy, and it remains very significant today even if less central. In India it has never achieved that same importance, although India's professed socialism had significant policy implications in the past, and has a constraining influence today. In both countries too nationalism is an important influence, and because of their present size and role, and their past history, it has a significant policy influence.

The industrial bureaucracies in both countries have interests independent from the governing parties and other groups in society, but the exercise of that interest differs between the two countries. In part this reflects the different relationship between party and bureaucracy in the two. A very important factor in the decision-making process is the relationship between the central power and the local or regional powers and interest. I will examine this factor in some detail later, since it differs between the two countries and has an important effect on their respective policies. Both countries are also peasant societies in terms of the bulk of their populations. This has implications as to relations among groups and individuals, accepted and expected exchanges among them, and expectations as to a ruler's economic responsibilities that the governing party must consider. These inevitably influence policy goals, the administration of policies, and the results of those policies.

The purpose of this comparison is not to determine whether one or the other country has a better system in some vague way. At one time it had been thought that the successes or failures of economic development in these two large countries with their different political systems would serve as models for other smaller developing countries and tilt the scales in favor of communism or democracy. But the experience of the past thirty years has certainly disproved that assumption. My interest in the contrast is for its own sake. This reflects first the importance of each of the countries, and the intrinsic interest of their attempts at policy change; second, the light their experience may throw on the process of economic reform or of making major changes in current economic policies in other countries, whether they may be dictatorships or democracies, developing or developed.

Each of the following chapters, until the final one, will explore a particular aspect of the reform process in China and India separately and conclude with an explicit comparison of the two with respect to that aspect.

Chapter 1 will briefly lay out the political economies of both countries, that is, the political, institutional, and ideological systems within which economic policy has been made since the reform periods began in each country. The purpose of this is to examine key aspects of the functioning of each country's political-economic system, which sets the framework for its industrial policy-making.

The second chapter will examine the functioning of each of the two industrial systems in the prereform periods to identify the pressures which led the policymakers to propose the economic reforms. This chapter will also outline the broad goals of those reforms.

This will be followed by two chapters on the economic reforms— the first summarizing the reforms, their sequencing, and the debates surrounding them, the second examining the economic results of the reforms in terms of such measures as output, trade, productivity, and welfare and in relation to their stated goals.

I will then specifically examine the relationship of the economic reforms and their results to the political economy of each country. This chapter will seek to identify how the broader political-economic system both contributed to each country's reforms and set limits to them as those economic reforms seemed to strengthen or threaten various aspects of each country's broader system. Did the political leaders believe that the system and the reforms in each country were mutually supportive? Or were the reforms felt to be undermining the political leadership? How did those perceptions influence the process of reform?

The final chapter will bring together the specific contrasts I have drawn in the earlier chapters, to draw broader comparisons of the directions of the reforms, their momentum, and their constraints. On the basis of this comparison I will try to draw implications for the future of reform in China and India, as well as some implications for the process of economic reform in other countries.

CHAPTER ONE

The Political-Economic Systems of China and India

Because we have too much liberty without any unity and resisting power, because we have become a sheet of loose sand and so have been invaded by foreign imperialism . . . [we] must break down individual liberty and become pressed together into an unyielding body like the firm rock which is formed by the addition of cement to sand.
SUN YAT-SEN, 1924

The most important external environment is the Government of India. You have to sell your ideas to the Government. Selling the idea is the most important thing, and for that I'd meet anybody in the Government. I am willing to salaam anyone. One thing you won't find in me, and that is an ego.
DHIRUBHAI AMBANI, industrialist, 1985

CHINA

IN this brief review of Chinese political economy I will focus on the characteristics of Chinese political and economic institutions in the Communist system to identify their potential influence in stimulating, shaping, and constraining the Chinese reform process.

China has been ruled by the dictatorship of its Communist party since 1949, functioning in terms of a Marxist ideology that had been interpreted by Lenin and Stalin in its application to the Soviet Union, and by Mao Zedong and Deng Xiaoping in its application to China. Marxism of course stresses the close relations among a country's productive structure, class system, and political structure. In feudal and capitalist societies the political system enables the dominant class to control the peasants and workers for the dominant class's benefit. In a socialist or a Communist state in which the workers have ostensibly achieved control, the Communist party both represents the workers

12

and governs the country on their behalf. In a country at a low level of economic development, in which the bulk of the population are peasants rather than industrial proletariat, the Communist party both rules on behalf of peasants and workers and has the responsibility of educating the people, raising their economic position and their awareness of their social position so that they will eventually be able to govern themselves in a truly Communist and classless society. Since private ownership of the means of production is a fundamental characteristic of capitalism that creates both the owning capitalist class and the exploited proletariat, one of the key characteristics of socialism, and of the final stage of communism, is that the means of production are owned by the state, which now represents all the people. They are administered by the Communist party, which governs directly on behalf of the workers and indirectly on behalf of all the people.

Not surprisingly, in China since 1949 there has been extensive debate within the Communist party, at times extending outside the party, as to the relations between the comparatively low level of development of the economy and the stage of socialism or communism. At issue are the appropriate methods and instruments to raise the level of China's productive forces; the class structure of a predominantly rural, nonindustrial society in which officials and intellectuals have traditionally played a significant role; and the appropriate role of the party in governing the country, administering the economy, and educating the people. The issue of the appropriate means, as well as the level, of exchange between the party leadership, the forty million party members, and the one billion Chinese people is also a subject of periodic debate. Both the processes and the results of the debate not only influence economic behavior and policies at the official level, but also affect popular motivations to work and the efforts the people are prepared to expend in their work.

Tang Tsou has pointed out that "policy debates [in China], particularly on the more fundamental and persistent issues, are couched or justified in terms of ultimate ideological principles. . . . Some of these [policy] issues are common to all developing countries such as the question whether to accord priority to economic growth over equality and participation or vice versa. . . . Other issues are pertinent to revolutionary regimes such as the question of whether to consolidate the revolutionary gains already achieved or to push the revolution further . . . or how a society can combine revolutionary change with stability and economic growth. Still other issues are relevant to Marxist regimes, such as whether a new class can emerge after the means of ownership have been socialized, what the basis of this new class is, and how to deal with it. There are also issues which are specific to China's response to the West but are also of [more] general relevance . . . such as the issue of self-reliance and the question of importance of technology and industrial plants."[1]

In the period of Mao Zedong's dominance of the party after 1949 there was one general direction of response to these issues: this response culminated in the Cultural Revolution and its aftermath. After Mao's death in September 1976, the overthrow of the "Gang of Four," the interim leadership of Hua Guofeng, and the rehabilitation and gradual rise to power of Den Xiaoping in 1977, the December 1978 meeting of the Third Plenum of the Eleventh Central Committee formally embarked upon another direction.

In the Mao period, especially after 1958, emphasis was placed upon ideology governing practice; upon the development of new classes or reincarnation of old bourgeois classes in the new governing groups of the party, the bureaucracy, and the managers and experts of industry, who intervene between the masses and the achievement of the equitable Communist society; upon the need for continuous revolution to overthrow the new ruling groups in order to permit the working classes and peasants to achieve their just position in the new society. This achievement in turn would lead to greater national effort and greater output. Mao's vision overcame the preference by such party leaders as Liu Shaoqi "for consolidation and incremental change . . . justified by emphasizing the limits imposed on human effort by the objective forces of production and by the need to develop production as a precondition for changes in social and economic institutions."[2]

Even before Mao's death, during Deng's temporary rehabilitation from 1973 to 1976, Deng was responsible for preparing a document in 1975 that argued that rising production was the prime necessity if Chinese society was to achieve the requirements for communism. In this document, study of theory and ideology was downgraded, the emphasis upon revolution rather than production was criticized, and a concrete program for raising production was presented. This concrete program "advocated the introduction of advanced technology, machinery and equipment from foreign countries. . . . [It] advocated the re-establishment of the 'responsibility system' under which every kind of work and every post . . . would have clearly defined responsibility [according to a] . . . system of rules and regulations. [It] sought to establish a strong and independent management and command system to run production with the Party committee exercising only general unified leadership . . . and refraining from the direct handling of matters large and small. [It] opposed 'absolute egalitarianism' and . . . proposed . . . 'a system of regular promotions and increase in wages.'"

That program also proposed a strong stress on the development of science and technology, arguing that "'philosophy cannot replace natural science' . . . in the field of science and technology, the dictatorship of the proletariat should not be mentioned . . . 'intellectuals are also laborers' . . . 'the role of specialists is underestimated.'" The study of technology, of works in foreign languages, and of professional literature should be encouraged if the "crisis" in science and technology was to be overcome.[3]

Mao's own response to this document was highly critical and contributed to the second expulsion of Deng from the inner circle and to his being passed over for the premiership and the leadership of the Communist party on the deaths of Chou Enlai and Mao himself in 1976. But that 1975 document clearly served as an introduction to the economic policies adopted once Deng achieved undisputed leadership of the party. Significantly too, one of the early actions of the post-Mao leadership of Hua and Deng was the publication in 1978 of the article "Practice Is the Sole Criterion for Testing Truth." This in effect signaled the start of a new debate on the relationship between ideology and practice, with ideology now subordinated to results.

While there have been major changes in various aspects of the relationship of ideology and policies since 1976, the Chinese political leadership which carried through those changes in policy and practice remains committed to the Four Principles: "upholding socialism, the dictatorship of the proletariat, the leadership of the party and Marxism-Leninism, and Mao Zedong thought. . . . It is clear that even the Cultural Revolution did not shake the faith of the veteran leaders in [these] basic ideological principles, and they cannot envisage an alternative system that will better perform the tasks of modernizing China. They have too much at stake. For many years . . . the question will be whether a political system set within these limits can . . . [promote] controlled social change fast enough to satisfy the demands and pressures originating inside China."[4]

Although the veteran leaders of the party may be fully convinced of the validity of the Four Principles in broad terms, the effect of the Cultural Revolution upon the relations between the larger public and the party has been profound. The Cultural Revolution was characterized by open conflict within the Communist party, the disgrace of the old leadership, conflict among the various identified public groups within Chinese society, the undermining of old relationships and the establishment of new relationships in the work unit, school, and neighborhood, apparent deliberate manipulation of group loyalties and conflicts for political advantage and the introduction of the army into the political process, and the deliberate victimization of the intellectuals and specialists who had played a supportive role in the revolution or who had volunteered their support to the new regime. It resulted in "demoralization, resentment, cynicism and frustrated hopes" in large parts of the population, both among the young, who were often the instruments of the violence, and the old, who were frequently its victims. This disillusion created a popular climate receptive to economic reform and change. It also led to a political party weakened and significantly discredited among large sections of the public and a distrust of former ideological principles and goals.[5] "[After] the Cultural Revolution the idea of reform had become unstoppable . . . 'without it, we could never have undertaken such a fundamental reform. It took the Cultural Revolution for us to realize the weaknesses of our old system.'"[6]

Hua Guofeng and Deng Xiaoping both saw economic improvement and greater economic well-being as a political goal—one whose achievement not only would contribute to century-long national goals and meet the demands of the public for an improvement in the conditions of living, but would once more justify the 1949 Revolution and the leading role of the Communist party after the disaster of the Cultural Revolution. The economic goal of quadrupling China's output by the year 2000 thus has a higher political objective. Its achievement would create the socialist society which is an intermediate step to the ultimate Communist society—in Deng's words, one "in which there is no exploitation . . . there is great material abundance and the principle from each according to his ability, to each according to his needs applies." Such abundance is to be achieved in the socialist stage, the task of which is "to develop the productive forces so as to provide the material basis for communism." For such a development economic reforms are necessary, but those reforms cannot be seen as undermining socialism; a "socialist economy [is] based on public ownership . . . [and in it] there must be no polarization of rich and poor. . . . [Any] bourgeois elements [that] may appear . . . will not form a class."

Reforms are risky, but the risks can be limited by "the socialist state apparatus . . . [that] is so powerful that it can intervene to correct any deviations [from socialism]. . . . The open policy [in particular] entails risks. Some decadent bourgeois things may be brought into China. But with our socialist policies and state apparatus we shall be able to cope with them." The main instrument to cope with these risks is the Communist party, which leads and controls the state apparatus. It is the party, united in its faith in Marxism and communism, and strictly disciplined to maintain its ideological unity and purity, that has to "promote cultural and ideological progress . . . that must undergird the economic progress of socialism." Improving party conduct is the key to improving general social conduct; part of that party conduct must be opposition to "propaganda in favor of bourgeois liberalization, that is . . . the capitalist road."

The party's discipline and ideological purity is necessary for the dictatorship which is required in China. "[Without] exercising dictatorship over . . . saboteurs, we cannot maintain political stability and unity or succeed in the modernization drive. . . . The dictatorship can ensure the smooth progress of . . . socialist modernization and deal effectively with persons [who undermine the work]."[7] In addition to dealing with the potential saboteurs, the dictatorship of a disciplined united party also "enables us to make quick decisions, while if we place too much emphasis on a need for checks and balances problems may arise. . . . [In 1980 the National People's Congress deleted] from the Constitution the provision concerning the right of citizens to 'speak out freely, air their views fully, hold great debates and put up big-character posters.'. . . If 'liberalization' had . . . spread, it would have undermined our political stability and unity, without which construction would be out of the question."[8]

Following the student demonstrations of December 1986 Deng restressed his opposition to "bourgeois liberalization" and emphasized the need for dictatorship. "There is no way to ensure continued political stability and unity without the people's democratic dictatorship. . . . Without leadership by the Communist Party and without socialism there is no future for China. . . . Bourgeois liberalization would plunge the country into turmoil again. [It] would mean rejection of the Party's leadership; there would be nothing to unite our one billion people, and the Party itself would lose all power to fight . . . [and] to lead the people in construction. . . . If our country were plunged into disorder and our nation reduced to a heap of loose sand, how could we ever prosper? The reason the imperialists were able to bully us in the past was precisely that we were a heap of loose sand. . . . China must take its own road and build socialism with Chinese characteristics. We must show foreigners that China's political situation is stable. . . . Without political stability and unity it would be impossible for us to go on with construction [and reform] let alone . . . the open policy. . . . During the 'cultural revolution' we had . . . mass democracy. . . . [When] the masses were roused to headlong action, the result was civil war. We have learned our lesson from history."[9]

What does democratization then mean in the Chinese context

as far as Deng is concerned? It is not "bourgeois democracy . . . the democracy of monopoly capitalists. . . . [It is a] people's democracy under the leadership of the Communist Party. . . . [Its] greatest advantage is that when the central leadership makes a decision it is promptly implemented without interference from other quarters. . . . We don't have to go through a lot of repetitive discussion and consultation. . . . From this point of view our system is very efficient. . . . We have superiority in [overall efficiency] . . . and we should keep it. In terms of [narrower] administration and economic management the capitalist countries are more efficient . . . in many respects. China is burdened with bureaucratism."[10]

What must China do in the way of political reform then? Deng lays down three steps: (1) revitalize the party and state by bringing in younger cadres, with fresh ideas and knowledge; (2) increase efficiency by reducing bureaucracy, which includes streamlining the party and government agencies and separating their functions so that the party deals with major issues while government agencies and enterprises can deal with their own specialized activities; (3) stimulate people's initiative by delegating power to lower levels, as in the rural reform. But socialist democracy cannot be based upon some vague "humanism, the value of the human being and so forth in abstract terms. . . . [Neither] in capitalist society nor in socialist society can there be an abstract . . . humanism, because even in our society there are still bad people, dregs of both the old and new societies, enemies of socialism and spies."[11]

Deng's remarks make clear the close relationship between China's political system and the policies of economic reform. The leading role of the Communist party and the need for a dictatorship of the party is repeatedly stressed. That need is not only in terms of ideology, but in practical terms to insure proper social conduct within which economic reform takes place, and to prevent the chaos that a Western-type democracy or freedom of criticism and speech threatens. The economic reform policy, including opening to the world, also implies certain risks: a movement toward capitalism and away from the public ownership which is the essence of socialism could create politically unacceptable income and class differences; and a movement toward bourgeois liberalism could result not only in capitalism, but in delays in decision-making, and ultimately, in chaos.

Dorothy Solinger, in her analysis of the ideological debate among the party's leaders over goals and methods and the party's role, emphasizes the continuous struggle among the three competing goals of egalitarianism, order, and productivity. This conflict has set the framework for Chinese industrial policy and contributes to the sharp shifts among "incompatible policies" as one or the other of these values has been pushed to the extreme.

> Maximum concentration on productivity often requires incentives that give short shrift to egalitarianism; and it also demands a flexibility for the play of market forces, which runs in the face of tight planning. . . . [The] approach to the promotion of equity through mass movements and disregard for centralized plans has spawned much disorder; whereas more orderly bureaucratic solutions tend to enhance the power of those at the upper levels . . . and thereby to reduce equality. . . . [Rigidities], waste, inefficiency and inability to serve demand effectively which characterize bureaucratic business, plus the tendency to play down material incentives [an approach that bureaucrats share with radicals], have several times paved the way for the release of market forces. . . .
>
> [The] illicit profit seeking and price increases that have accompanied this market-type release then provoke and legitimize once again the radical profession of egalitarian ideals. . . . [Thus as] each [of these three often contradictory goals] is carried out to its limit, the economic consequences trigger an elite reaction which leads to policy shift.[12]

In her opinion the underlying tendency among these shifts has been toward planned, bureaucratically organized decision making. A major factor favoring this tendency is the existence of a large economic bureaucracy with its own interests, relationships, and habits, which prefers such an orderly, controlled approach.

Ideology and party role are key issues of political economy associated with Communist party rule in China. But there are also various long-standing relationships within Chinese society that influence the making of policy. One of the most important of these is the relationship between the central government and the governance of China's widely dispersed regions and provinces. This relationship does not revolve around ethnic issues, except perhaps with regard to Tibet. It is mainly associated with China's sheer size, the relatively poor communications within the country, and the resulting difficulty of centralized rule of such a large country from Beijing, as well as with China's pre-Communist history. The Communist rule followed a lengthy period of civil war, invasion, and provincial warlordism during which the power of the central government was restricted in its geographic reach. But quite apart from that lengthy period of turmoil, the boundaries of the administrative divisions of contemporary China—especially counties and provinces—were "historically de-

termined. They result from repeated social interaction that was established well before modernization, and [these boundaries] are
likely to describe a local economy, communications network and political culture." The party cadres staffing the "pre-modern hierarchy
of administrative-territorial units . . . since 1949 . . . have developed
[an] . . . administrative style and political skills based on that hierarchy." There may well be a possible "contradiction between the
political and economic imperatives of the old and new order respectively, at least in the short term." In imperial China in order to reduce
the conflict between local loyalties and central direction there was a
deliberate policy of assigning officials elsewhere than their native
provinces, and of transferring them frequently. Today there is not
such a policy; rather there is some effort to balance natives with out-
siders in local leadership posts, and a reliance upon Communist party
membership, and inspection visits from Beijing, to achieve confor-
mity to central policy.[13]

Initially under Mao there was centralizing pressure that reflected
the adopted Soviet model of centralized planning and allocation of inputs and outputs to achieve the goal of large-scale industrial development centering on the iron and steel industry. That goal in turn
contributed to deliberate policy to tap natural resources in remote
areas of the country, either by establishing industrial complexes
around such resources, or improving transport facilities from mines
and oil wells to existing plants. By the mid-1960s every provincial
capital except Lhasa had its own medium- or large-scale iron and steel
plant.

Two major factors contributed to the subsequent decentralization of the country's industry by Mao. These were the security fears
of the 1960s and Mao's ideological antibureaucratic preferences for
local initiatives, expressed in the Great Leap Forward and the Cultural Revolution. In the 1960s and 1970s an "overriding objective of
[the regionalization] policy was to furnish the interior provinces with
their own basic industrial infrastructure in order that they might
stand alone in the event of external attack or internal counter-
revolution." The area of Sichuan and its neighbors to the south, east,
and north was the heart of this inner security region. It is estimated
that over half of China's investment in fixed capital assets in the
period between roughly 1964 to 1976 occurred within that area as part
of the security program, and that this investment resulted in the establishment of 29,000 state enterprises employing sixteen million
workers.[14]

There was also a great emphasis by Mao upon local "self reliance," as part of his effort to increase grass-roots involvement in the

decision-making process, breaking the bureaucratic influences and inertia. This led to efforts at provincial self-sufficiency, the goal of "small but complete," and to the duplication of "fashionable" types of enterprises—iron and steel, motor vehicles, chemicals—in neighboring provinces, and barriers to trade in those products among provinces.

A consequence of the mixed goals and policies on this issue has been the sharp swings from a high degree of central control over industry to the delegation of powers of control and allocation to provincial and local governments, which however has led to problems of coordination and to a reimposition of central powers.[15] Since the Great Leap Forward of the early 1960s there has been "dispersed industrialization and decentralized, or even fragmented, economic administration. The result is the prevalence of small enterprises on the one hand and a close relationship between the local government and enterprises extending well beyond formal planning on the other. . . . Interference in enterprises is essential for the functioning of the government and enterprises need the support of local government to operate." This relationship is largely outside the central plan.[16]

In the early stages of Communist rule the relations between the central and local administrations had been bridged by the party and its leading role at all levels. But over time obvious errors of central directives applied to the local scene led to a withering of that relationship. (One hears of numerous disastrous cropping results in various local areas arising from errors in central directives combined with a reluctance of local authorities to challenge these errors. The national disasters during the Great Leap Forward were one consequence.) Apart from such results of overcentralization, the separate development and financial interests of the various levels of government, complicated by the differing interests of enterprise managers and workers, led to the growth of a complex negotiating system among these various layers of administrative and party officials.

Under Mao the movement toward local self-reliance extended down to the county commune level. In Vivienne Shue's words, "the commune was explicitly conceived as a highly self-contained unit, in which economic life, social life, and political authority were fused in a single, comprehensive organization. . . . [Communes] had little lateral intercourse with one another. The same principle applied to counties. . . . The markets served by rural industries built in the thrall of the 'self-reliance' effort were usually highly localized and quickly saturated. . . . [The] product variety was limited, and product quality was unreliable. . . . But trade of all sorts with other units was to be avoided."[17]

The local cadres sought to protect their community from the demands of the center and provinces, as well as to develop the community they governed in the way they thought most appropriate for local interests as well as for their own. "They deliberately dug in their heels during tough negotiations with superior officials on matters that affected local welfare and development. . . . [They] calculated how to bend the rules of the state-planned economy . . . to serve local interests even as they were *enhancing their own power* within the system. Their goal most often was . . . [to construct] independent local economic bases under their own control." Shue goes on to give an example of one North China county which was successful in increasing the proportion of expenditures controlled by the county officials from 1.2 percent in 1959 to 30 percent in 1977.[18] Other evidence of the ability of local cadres to take actions to further local interests is shown in the growth of the number of county- and commune-owned enterprises, even though these were restricted and attacked as "the tail of capitalism." By 1978 there were over 1.5 million such local small enterprises collectively owned by the county or commune, employing twenty-eight million workers.[19]

In addition to such problems of direct central-local control relations at the microeconomic level, China lacks an effective indirect macroeconomic control system with experienced administrators managing financial macroinstitutions. There is neither an effective central bank nor a nationwide banking system under the control of such a bank. In a Stalinist type of centrally planned economy such indirect instruments are unnecessary since all transactions are controlled directly through the central budget and by the supply of funds to enterprises in line with planned uses. But as direct controls are lifted, the absence of indirect tools can lead to macroeconomic problems of inflation or foreign exchange losses that can be met only by reimposition of direct controls. Theoretically, too, the absence of a role for an interest rate or an interest rate policy or of any macroeconomic theory in traditional Marxist analysis has made the introduction of macroeconomic policies and instruments ideologically difficult. In addition, where local banks have been introduced, the power of local officials may lead to the use of such institutions by local party leaders as instruments in their own political or economic networks, irrespective of broader national interests. Thus while the economic bureaucracy may be a factor for order in the system, there are counterfactors within that bureaucracy that make for disorder and complexity.

Finally there are certain characteristics of China's traditional and peasant society that inevitably continue since the Revolution, because China has remained a largely peasant society in terms of population and employment. These in turn impinge upon the implementation of broader economic policies, including industrial policies. Among such characteristics are the importance of familial relationships in influencing economic actions among family members; of patron-client relationships in influencing relations within a group, although patrons and clients may have changed after the revolution (e.g., the patron role shifting from local landlord to party secretary); of traditional hierarchical relationships which give the government official and intellectual high status in society, while the producer of goods and merchants have a lower status; and of a gift-obligation relationship between patron and client that may extend to higher and lower members of the hierarchy. There are also accepted moral dimensions of equity and security that exist in a peasant society and that continue as expectations even as that society industrializes and modernizes in the process of development. Such complex social relations establish a framework within which the peasant society functions. While a revolution may overthrow that framework, there is no guarantee that elements of it will not continue below the surface and become implicitly reestablished, when and if revolutionary momentum diminishes and disillusionment replaces ideological fervor.[20]

INDIA

India is a democracy that has proved its effectiveness in the political sphere as recently as 1989, when the long-ruling Congress party was defeated by a coalition of opposition parties. I have already pointed out some of the political characteristics of that democracy: a variety of parties with representatives in the national and state legislatures, which controlled many of the state governments for lengthy periods; a free press; and an effective constitution and legal system. The Constitution, in addition to stating the basic rights of the people and expressing the basic goals of the society, establishes a broad tripartite division of powers among the executive, legislative, and judicial branches of the government, and defines the respective spheres of the central and state governments. These of course have been further defined by the experience of the forty-odd years since independence. In economic policy the center is in general dominant. However the state governments have major power with regard to the agricultural sector of the economy, and more specifically with respect to such matters as land reform and land tax policy. (However prices of inputs to and outputs of the agricultural sector are frequently set by the center.) The state governments also control such economically important matters as the distribution of electric power and education. The center largely controls sources of fiscal revenue and the allocation of revenues from major tax sources to the states for development purposes. In addition India has a centralized and well-organized institutional system, based on the Ministry of Finance and the Reserve Bank of India, for developing and implementing macroeconomic policies. Both these agencies have lengthy experience in the macroeconomic sector.

One strain of ideas underlying the constitutional system and broad administrative structure reflects the influence of Western political and economic ideas upon the leaders of the Congress party, which led the fight for independence against Britain. This influence was transmitted through education and example, as well as by such direct administrative instruments as the Indian Civil Service (ICS), with its bureaucratic traditions and practices at the peak of the bureaucracy—and with a status only half jokingly compared to that of the Brahmins in the Hindu caste system. The ICS was in effect converted into the Indian Administrative Service (IAS), after independence. But the IAS is today an instrument of a democratically elected political leadership, not of an imperial power wielding what, in the last analysis, was dictatorial rule.

Since independence the Indian component in the functioning of that system has become dominant. One element of that component is what P. N. Dhar calls India's unique political style—one that "emphasizes reconciliation of differences through compromise and accommodation [and which] avoids confrontation and seeks consensus." This has contributed to a broad continuity of economic policy in India since independence. There has been "an arrangement which retained the free market of capitalism [while it] . . . widened the sphere of public ownership . . . [and thereby] avoided ideological collision and social upheavals."[21] A significant strain of the Indian ideology was what Raj Krishna calls an "Indianised version of the 19th century Fabianism." This was the basis of Nehru's ideology, and in turn that of the "entire [Indian] intelligentsia maturing in the Nehru period." An underlying element of that ideology is a vision of the state as an agency of, and for, the whole people so long as "the full democratic process is available." In the broad political-economic area the policy implications of that ideology for India were:

> 1) The State shall own and/or manage the heavy [industry], infrastructure and financial sectors (the commanding heights of the economy). [The 1948 Industrial Policy Resolution divided the industrial sector itself into three parts: one reserved for the

state; a second in which private and public enterprises might coexist; and the third, a residual, for private ownership.]

2) Permitted private activity shall be regulated by the State to the extent considered necessary with respect to investment, access to key inputs and credits, production, prices, profits, wages and working conditions.

3) Universal franchise in a poverty-stricken mass society will throw up governments increasingly committed to the eradication of poverty and social injustice.

4) The system of administration, inherited from the British, suitably reformed and made accountable to the elected civil leadership will remain an effective instrument for . . . running a democratic socialist regime.

The state-owned industrial sector in turn was expected to prevent concentration of wealth and income, generate a surplus for reinvestment, provide for mass needs at low cost, and set modern employment standards.[22]

Central planning was a major instrument to implement this vision of democratic socialism, which would achieve an industrialized, modern India, with its people living at a significantly higher level and far more equitably than in the past. But it is consistent with P. N. Dhar's picture of India's system as one of compromise and consensus that even before independence some of India's largest private industrialists had proposed their Bombay Plan, which had marked similarities to the ideas of India's Second Five-Year Plan. The British government in India had also prepared a plan for India's postwar development, and the British wartime economic administrative mechanism and control system provided a basis for India's economic control system after independence.

The Congress party under Nehru's influence had been working on draft plans in the 1930s. The First Five-Year Plan was introduced in 1951, but primarily as a symbolic statement; the second (1956) and third (1961) plans were a product of extended research and expert economic opinion from both Indian and foreign economists focused on achieving the goals of India's political leaders. These two plans laid the basis of many of India's economic policies for the next three decades. In Dhar's opinion those policies reflected Nehru's social democratic ideas, modified by Gandhian concerns and India's needs as an "industrializing and underdeveloped country."[23]

Reflecting Nehru's ideas, priority was given to industrial development of the basic and capital goods industries. The government was to set up these enterprises, and own and manage them. Import substitution was a major instrument of industrialization on grounds of a

reasoned pessimism with respect to exports based on the experience
of the 1930's to conserve foreign exchange for priority purposes; and it
was a step toward the goal of economic independence. A licensing
system was established to control the growth of the private sector to
prevent diversion of capital resources from those priority sectors and
to limit monopoly trends.

Mahatma Gandhi's ideas did not affect those basic policy goals,
but they had a stronger influence on the policies and actions aimed at
protecting existing employment and generating additional employment, by encouraging handicraft industries in general, and the hand-
spinning and weaving of textiles in particular, as opposed to the
modern factory enterprises that might be competitive to them.
Greater demands were expected for such goods by final consumers
with higher incomes arising from the large investments in the late-
yielding capital goods industries proposed in the Second Plan.
Gandhi's ideas contributed to the rationale of relying on small-scale
and handicraft industries for the production of those goods. Thus India's lead in the development and protection of small-scale industries
was influenced by Gandhian ideas. Another strain of Gandhi's influence, which supported Nehru's emphasis upon capital goods development but also drew support from a British upperclass distrust of
ostentation, was a negative attitude toward consumerism on moral
grounds apart from economic grounds. People should live simply and
neither accumulate nor display their wealth in the form of consumer
goods. Thus while there was an underlying belief in democratic socialism, there were sufficient other elements in the mix of ideologies
and sufficient compromise among the proponents of those elements
to avoid the rigidities and fierce conflicts that characterized Chinese
policy-making.

Another major element in India's political economy, as in
China's, has arisen from its great geographical spread; but in India, far
more so than in China, this has been accompanied by major ethnic,
religious, and language differences among the different areas of the
newly established country.

> [The] formation of the State and the consolidation of the coun-
> try and its economic development had to take place
> concurrently. . . . Given the size and diversity of India and its
> fractious history, the convergence [of the formation of the state
> and economic development] had to be politically engineered and
> for this some economic price had to be paid.
>
> It would be possible, in a more homogeneous country, to
> give the highest priority to growth, but not in a country of In-
> dia's diversity. . . . [Problems] arose, and continue to arise, on

account of the uneven distribution of resources and differential levels and rates of development in different parts of the country. Furthermore, the natural economic or geographical units that could be carved out for developmental purposes are not coterminous with the boundaries of the linguistic states . . . [of] the Union of India. The factors result in conflicts between national, regional and sub-regional economic goals. . . . [There have been serious conflicts over the utilization of river waters and over the distribution of industrial investments, and these have led to long delays in desirable projects, and to clearly uneconomic locations of major investment.] This was the price paid for the consolidation of the country and the creation of a national socio-economic base for the State. . . . Economic planning in federal India has to be a series of balancing acts between conflicting national, regional and sub-regional goals which reduce the level of its efficiency in comparison with that of a smaller and more homogeneous country.[24]

The policy framework of the 1950s and early 1960s was subsequently implemented by specific legislation against monopoly, by nationalization of banks, and by extension of the protection of small-scale industry. Within that policy framework and in light of the regional constraints indicated above, India from about 1950 to 1980 achieved a steady but modest annual rate of growth of real total national income on the order of 3.5–4.0 percent, and of per capita income of 1.5–2.0 percent, which Raj Krishna dubbed "the Hindu rate of growth." But associated with that rate of growth have been the achievements of "a diversified economy, impressive gains in food-grain production, vast increases in trained manpower, expanded technological capabilities, and an increased rate of domestic savings. . . . India does now produce most of its earlier [industrial] imports, and in that sense . . . has achieved [a large measure of industrial] self-reliance."[25] It was these economic achievements that contributed to continued public support in the form of election victories for the Congress party of Nehru, and later, of his daughter.

India's combination of a political democracy, a large government-owned industrial sector and infrastructure tightly controlled by government agencies of one type or another, and a private sector functioning within a complex and very elaborate system of controls, by the early 1980s had resulted in a unique political-economic system dominated by the state at the central level. The elaborate control network over private industrial enterprise encouraged the exchange of permissions sought by business firms for political funds to the Congress and other governing parties, as well as direct payments to numerous bureaucratic and political intermediaries at various levels of

government. Some business figures used their political and bureaucratic contacts to manipulate the system to prevent entry of possible competitors into their fields, or to corner undervalued items and
foreign exchange in short supply, to later sell them in a higher priced
gray market. With the tight import controls, the smuggling of many
consumer durable goods, as well as other items, became usual. A
thriving "second economy" grew alongside the legal one; it was estimated by one study to be about one-fifth the size of the legal one.

In the public sector itself, not surprisingly, economic and political decision making are interrelated. Location decisions of public-
sector plants have political consequences and are made in the light of
those consequences. Political criteria play a significant role in the ap-
pointment of senior management, and lower staff appointments have
been rumored to require cash payments. The large public-sector trade
unions are politically important, often affiliated with political parties, and play major roles in preventing reductions in "surplus" labor
and limiting management powers as they might affect labor-force productivity. Trade unions, in order to prevent unemployment, at times
prevent the closure of inefficient publically owned plants, and bring
pressure on the government to support or take over private plants that
might be facing bankruptcy.

The large number of businessmen and workers in the small-scale
industry sector make it one of the strongest political pressure groups
in the country, especially at the state level. The strength of this pressure group is often used to increase concessions, such as credit, of-
fered to small-scale industry, to prevent any reduction in those
concessions, and to fight both enforcement of existing legislation and
introduction of more stringent laws in such areas as child labor that
would threaten that sector's profitability. And many of these groups,
whether in large or small industry, often unite against the import of
foreign products or direct foreign investment that appears to be com-
petitively threatening.

In summary, the demand groups in the governing and industrial
sectors of the Indian population who have benefited by their positions in this state-dominated industrial system include: (1) political
figures at every level whose intermediation may be necessary for a
decision on an economic issue; (2) the administrators who make
many of the formal decisions; (3) the large-scale private industrialists
whose profits are influenced by their ability to manipulate the controls in their favor; (4) the many small-scale businessmen, more numerous than the larger-scale ones, whose continued existence may
depend on their concessions and reservations; and (5) the workers in
the trade unions in the large public- and private-sector plants who use

their political clout to protect their jobs and advantages by protecting the enterprises in which they work. Demand groups of course also exist in the farm sector, but these are of only marginal interest for this analysis.[26]

Apart from the control system itself, another major connection between the political system and the identified demand groups is through the central and state budgets in the form of subsidies targeted to the demand groups. The great increase in these subsidies between 1960 and 1982 is a clear sign of the growing importance of the demand groups in the polity. In fiscal year 1982–83 (the Indian fiscal year extends from April 1 to March 30) the total of direct subsidies granted by both central and state governments was forty times greater than the 1960–61 figure, without including the subsidized losses of public-sector enterprises. In 1980–81 the sum of central government subsidies on (1) prices of food sold to urban inhabitants at below the purchase prices paid to farmers; (2) on prices of fertilizer bought by those farmers; and (3) on prices of exported industrial products and paid to the industrial firms producing the exports equaled half of the total investment in public-sector manufacturing. Apart from such subsidies, as a result of the relatively rapid growth of government employment and the comparatively higher incomes of government employees, the service sector of the economy has shown significantly higher rates of growth than the commodity producing sectors—agriculture and industry—during the 1960–86 period. This great increase in the level of administrative expenditures and subsidies, together with the higher level of defense expenditures after the fighting with China in late 1962, has inevitably meant that a smaller share of nondebt revenue is available for public investment for development. Government revenues from taxes and public-sector profits have also grown at a much lower rate than expenditures. These trends have led to greater reliance on deficit financing and the creation of money to finance both investment and current spending, which in turn has fueled a generally rising price level averaging close to 10 percent per year since Nehru's death.[27]

The growing importance of these demand groups is paralleled by the changing character of the political system and more directly of the Congress party itself. Before independence, under the leadership of Mahatma Gandhi, Nehru, and V. Patel, and then in the Nehru years, it was a political force dedicated to independence and later to the development and equity goals of democratic socialism. Internally it was a party with roots that extended to the local level as a result of a democratic process of choosing those leaders at both local and national levels, and of exchanging ideas on policies and their implementation among members at various levels. But following the deaths of Nehru and his immediate successor, L. B. Shastri, with the subsequent rise of Indira Gandhi, after a struggle for power between her and the old leadership, and the splits in the Congress, the democratic character of the party disappeared. Local leaders, state leaders, and national party leaders were chosen unilaterally and dismissed unilaterally by the prime minister and the close circle of officials around her (including her sons). Conflicts were over power, and ideas and policies played a subordinate role. At the local level too leaders were wooed and chosen for their control over "vote banks" held together by caste or ethnic ties or by patron-client relations; in addition local thugs were recruited for their power and willingness to do as they were asked, if they were paid enough in one form or another. Large financial support for campaigning and operation of the Congress was necessary, and business contributions, in exchange for desired actions, became a major element of electoral financing, not only for the Congress party, but for competitive parties, whether on a national or state level. A market was established for government favors at both the central and state levels in exchange for financial support for the governing party.

The limits of such a system are seen when we look at the spread of the benefits of the economic development that has in fact occurred. One of the assumptions of the Nehrovian vision was that democracy and elections in India would eventually lead to governments committed to political and economic steps to reduce and eventually eliminate poverty. Indira Gandhi recognized this in her battles for power with the older party leadership by pushing for such populist steps as nationalization of the banks and antimonopoly legislation. This culminated in the 1971 parliamentary elections when she campaigned on a promise to abolish poverty, which helped her Congress party to win a two-thirds majority of the seats.

But the promise has not been fulfilled. Part of that failure reflects the sheer magnitude of the goal, but it also reflects the functioning of the system. Dhar estimates that of India's 800 million people the number of those in the politically potent demand groups and able to use their influence to substantially improve their well-being, within the bounds of a 3.5–4.0 percent overall growth rate for the economy, is about 100–125 million.[28] Thus the gains of development have trickled down only marginally to the great majority of Indians. There has probably been some marginal improvement in the condition of farm laborers in those regions where agricultural productivity has increased dramatically, and by such direct antipoverty programs as the Integrated Rural Development Poverty program which aims to shift resources to poor farm families. (The IRDP program sought to provide 15 million low-income farm families with additional resources that would enable them to improve their productivity and raise incomes.)[29] Possibilities for upward mobility have also opened up for those groups and individuals that were able to take advantage of education and job reservations for scheduled and backward castes and tribes. The ending of widespread famine is of course a major achievement.

But even with these efforts, there is general agreement that from one-third to one-half of the country's population remains below the biologically determined poverty income line. While that proportion may have fallen somewhat since 1960 (though even that is questionable if the higher proportion is correct), the absolute number of people below that line has probably risen as India's population has grown at over 2 percent per year since then. In addition some groups have seen their position worsened by deforestation and other environmental damage.[30] While there are elements within the Indian political economic system that make change a difficult and complex process, the existence of democracy with its periodic elections creates pressure, at least at election times, to promise actions that will benefit the majority of the people, and later to take actions to fulfill some of those promises, or to risk loss at the next vote. The existence of a system with relatively open information and criticism has also greatly increased the numbers of voters not only in the cities but in the villages who are aware of some of these issues.

Finally in India, as in China, there are strong elements of a traditional peasant society that places many relations among individuals within a family framework, and among families within a patron-client system of mutual obligations. But the peasant society also has a set of expectations as to what is a desirable way of living and what are the respective duties of a patron, whether a landlord, a manager, or a political figure, and of a client. These expectations of what a good life should be and what appropriate behavior is influence not only individual economic behavior, but also how an individual will vote, and how the elected official will behave after the election.[31]

SOME CONTRASTS BETWEEN POLITICAL ECONOMIES

A basic difference that Chinese commentators have noted is that with China's one-party rule decisions have been made quickly in contrast to a more democratic system with limitation on institutional change. But while this does make for speed and flexibility, it has also

made, in China, for sharp swings in policy, reflecting ideological conflicts among the leadership and swings among those who control at
any given moment. In China these have made for extremes of policy
and goals; the results of the shifts have been rapid movement in the
directions adopted, whether those be toward greater equity or more
rapid growth, until they hit an obstacle arising from the neglected
goal. Under Mao those shifts were convulsive because they reflected
the shifting ends and position of one leader; under Deng they have
been less convulsive because there is some need for a consensus
among the top leadership. But those swings continue in part because
the revolution destroyed the intermediary institutions that might
have made transitions more gradual as problems arose and were recognized by the political leadership.

In India there has always been democratic leadership within an
elaborate constitutional network, and this has made for continuity of
policy within a broad socialistic consensus. This has resulted in fairly
steady economic growth at a slow average pace, somewhat below the
Chinese growth rate. India's achievement in the areas of poverty reduction and equity, health, and literacy has lagged behind China's on
average, but there have been no famines, and little of the political persecution that has characterized China's recent history. The leaders of
the India Congress party, and of the national government, including
Nehru and his daughter, have been constrained by the powers and interests of the states, especially in the field of agricultural policy,[32] but
the Indian states have less industrial and financial power than the
Chinese provinces and localities. In addition India's socialism has
never had the ideological purity or the militancy of China's communism with the resulting sharp conflicts over, and swings in, policy.
This relative continuity of policy in India has been balanced by a
slower response to change, which has advantages but which also
could have some disadvantages in responding to crises (although in
general India has responded well to emergencies, in part because they
can be, and are, exposed by a free press).

In both countries the bureaucracies have been forces for continuity of policies and institutions. In China the role of the party over
the bureaucracy has contributed to shifts in practice as party goals
have changed. In India the bureaucracy represents an element in the
system in some part independent of party control in fact as well as
theory, and this too has made for stability. India too, has had a network of control institutions, such as the Central Bank, that China
had abolished before 1980.

Both China and India regarded themselves as socialist, with the
implication of a dominant role for the government over the economy.

In China that role was all-encompassing; in India it was dominant but exercised through control of private economic activity in the agricultural sector by prices, subsidies, and investment, and in the industry sector by tight regulation, some price-setting, and investment.

In both countries too regional and local interests have been strong, reflecting past history, large geographic expanses, and sharp ethnic and linguistic differences, especially in India. In China the central government exercised its control via the Communist party and its leadership, whose power reached to all areas of the country. Initially under Mao, that power was very strong; but even under Mao regional differences and local interests expressed themselves in practice, and under his successors they became stronger. In India regional differences and interests were always strong, but in the economic field the central government's powers dominated the state governments by virtue of the Constitution and the country's institutional macroeconomic control framework. Both of these elements were largely absent in China, so that their center-regional economic relations were more a product of bargaining than they were in India.

Finally, both countries still had large elements of the traditional relations of a peasant society, in terms of patron-client attitudes, attitudes toward the place of money-making as opposed to other types of activity, and expectations of a good life. These attitudes and expectations influenced the behavior of government and party officials, as well as of private individuals dealing with the former, thus influencing government policies and their results in both countries. This book is an exploration of the interrelations of these various economic, political (including ideological), regional, and traditional forces and pressures, which determined the different styles of economic policy-making and the changing policies in China and India during the decade of the 1980s, and the effect of those changes.

CHAPTER TWO

The Necessity for Economic Reform

Three things are essential to a nation: the first is the government, the second wealth, the third power. If a nation has good government, it can strive to achieve prosperity and strength. . . . The way to attain good government is to reform native institutions; the way to attain wealth and power is to adopt Western methods.

Memorial written by two Chinese officials in 1901

PROBLEMS OF CHINA'S INDUSTRIAL ECONOMY BEFORE THE REFORM

THE victory of the Chinese Communist party in 1949 ushered in the first extended period of political and economic stability in China since the fall of the Qing dynasty in 1912. Even prior to that collapse there had been significant internal unrest and foreign interference. But levels of instability increased markedly after 1912 with the greater loss of central control, extended warlordism and civil war, massive foreign invasion, and international war before the eventual Communist success in 1949. Once military victory was won the new government moved quickly both to solidify its political control and to stabilize the economy by controlling the runaway inflation. As noted previously, the government introduced sweeping reforms in both the agricultural and industrial sectors. In industry the Stalinist model of politically driven comprehensive central planning was introduced, with substantial advisory and economic assistance from the Soviet Union until 1960. The administration of that industrial system was modified even before the 1980 reforms by cycles of administrative decentralization to give more weight to local needs and initiatives and for security reasons, followed by renewed centralization in response to the problems arising from decentralization. But in

34

either case, industry was politically and administratively controlled, above the enterprise, from the 1950s to the early 1980s.[1]

In the East European version of this system, output targets for enterprises were set from the top down and presented to the managers in plans prepared by the central planning agency and the industrial ministries to which the firms were subordinate; inputs were allocated to enterprises in some estimated relationship to output targets; outputs were distributed by government trading agencies to intermediate and final consumers. Prices were set not on the basis of costs or demands, but on the basis of some presumed social desirability. An enterprise's performance was judged on its ability to meet its output targets; since prices were simply accounting records rather than economically significant indicators, the enterprise's financial performance was ignored. Financial shortfalls of the enterprise were made up from the government budget or by allocations through the banking system, which was completely subordinate to the plan-implementing bureaucracy. Investment was governed by the plan and was divorced from the firm's performance; funds for investment were automatically provided once the project was in the plan.

But in China the degree of centralization was far less than in the Soviet Union. At the height of centralization fewer than 600 goods were centrally allocated, and 10,000 enterprises were under central control—these were the peaks, both of which were rapidly followed by falls. (Those figures were also well below the equivalent Russian figures.) This was because the Chinese industrial economy was far different from that of the USSR and other socialist East European countries. China is estimated to have had approximately 435,000 industrial enterprises in 1984, a far greater figure than that in other socialist countries. Fewer than 1 percent of these were large, in the sense that they had more than 243 workers, compared to two-thirds in Hungary and one-third in Yugoslavia with more than that number of workers. The small plants produced about 40–50 percent of the gross value of China's industrial output before 1980. With such a large number of small firms, "the Chinese planning system has . . . evolved differently from those in Eastern Europe. . . . [The] impossibility of incorporating [the large numbers of small enterprises] into the planning structure led to the creation of a multitiered, regionally based system where much of the responsibility for planning and coordination devolved to local governments. . . . Large-scale key enterprises remained in the central plan, while non-key enterprises were left to planning and coordination at the provisional, prefectural and county levels. . . . In general, the share of enterprise output included in the central plan declines as we move down the enterprise hierarchy [in terms of size and central control]." Thus in 1977–78, when the central plan included 50–55 percent of the gross value of industrial output, while all of the output of the centrally administered large enterprises came under the central plan, only about one-half to two-thirds of the output of provincial and city enterprises, one-fourth to one-third of the output of county and prefectural enterprises, and finally one-fifth of the output of rural collectives was under the central plan.[2]

One author has compared the preparation of the Chinese national plan in such circumstances to a chess game, characterized by detailed exchanges and bargaining, upward and downward, among the various planning agencies. At the top there was the central plan agency, which was largely responsible for the long-term ten-year plan; then the provincial and municipal plan agencies were deeply involved with the central agency in preparing the five-year plan; and at the lowest level the county planning agencies and the enterprises themselves were involved in preparing annual operational plans which translated the longer-term goals and indices into immediate operational targets for the individual enterprises.[3]

The individual enterprises themselves were often under a complex and multilayered group of control agencies for their actual operations and decisions. As one example, in the late 1970s and early 1980s the Shenyang Smelter, a large nonferrous metals plant in northeast China, dealt with four different administrative levels: the national Ministry of Metallurgy (MM) set one level of output targets and allocated inputs accordingly. The Shenyang Metallurgy Bureau (SMB), which controlled the smelter formally, gave the smelter different output targets and profit targets, which were determined by revenue targets set for the SMB by the municipality and province; it also demanded social actions by the firm in such areas as housing and education. The SMB however did not have the technical expertise or control over inputs to influence effectively the enterprise on technology or outputs or investment plans. The provincial economic commission allocated electric power to the plant. In addition the organization department of the central committee of the Chinese Communist party had the final formal authority to appoint and remove the enterprise directors and party secretaries in the plant.[4]

This formal political power over the top operating and political officers in the Shenyang plant reflected the general power of the Communist party in all planning and decision-making enterprises. "The party committee [CPC] of the enterprise was responsible for integrating the individual enterprise into the national plan, . . . the party committee ensured that the enterprise reached the targets set for it according to the central plan. . . . The party committee had the power to make the most important decisions, but the factory director was responsible for the behavior of the employees as well as the effective functioning of the production process. Perhaps for this reason the manager tried to wear two hats . . . to be a member of management as well as to occupy an important position in the CPC committee. . . . The CPC . . . also became involved in coordination matters at the level above the enterprise. . . . First, the enterprise's party organization had actively to make contacts outward, as it was mainly responsible for the functioning of the firm. Second, with the decentralization of planning, the provincial and municipal level party committees gained much more power and responsibility." These generalizations are supported by detailed analyses of management practices in eight firms in 1980, which concluded that "the CPC committee of the enterprise was . . . the most powerful unit in the firm. If the general manager of the firm was at the same time the first secretary . . . of the enterprise CPC committee, he had concentrated influence very much in his hands. . . . When the general manager [combined the top party role] . . . , middle managers did not dare to make decisions independently, but waited for decisions from him, and thus the work had to wait also, which could cause great inefficiency."[5]

The effect of both the administrative control system, which was highly decentralized and very complex as a result, and the party rule within the enterprise was that the enterprise managers had no formal powers of control over the operations of their firms although they might bargain informally over the output targets and input allocations given to them. They "had to seek approval for doing everything big and small, from higher departments which . . . had no responsibility for the results of . . . operations . . . and [which] often gave impractical and disconnected mandatory directives."[6] Authorizations from above were required for even very small expenditures by the enterprise managers. As a result enterprise managing was considered a soft rather than taxing job, an attitude which was reinforced by the absence of any reward for effective managerial performance.

Perhaps more similar to the approach of the Soviet Union was that the centrally planned industrial policy centered on building up the investment goods industries—steel, capital equipment, machinery. Resources were invested in plants to produce such goods, and those resources were in large part earned by the producing plants. All revenues above costs were turned over to the government, and costs were kept low by keeping wages low. China's investment as a percentage of GNP was very high, in a range of 30–40 percent, but the results of such investment levels and policies were both low wages and a low availability of consumer goods on which workers could spend their earnings.

Another already noted characteristic of the industrial investment policy was the widespread dispersion of industrial plants, in part for reasons of defense, and in part for purposes of regional equity, which also reflected the power of the provinces. The direct and indirect costs of the defense program in terms of both low-yielding returns on the investment projects undertaken, and investments forgone, were very high.[7] Provinces also sought to achieve self-sufficiency in their own industrial production; interprovincial trade was discouraged and even prohibited in competing products; scale economies were not considered, or if thought of were ignored. The net effect was a substantial waste of capital investment with both an unnecessary duplication of production of many products and serious shortages of many intermediate and final products. Such imbalances encouraged firms to stockpile inputs that either were, in fact, in short supply, or for which a shortage was feared; and an informal barter of inputs and outputs grew up among firms seeking to build up unplanned stockpiles of such products. Technological change was generally neglected, since such changes might reduce a firm's ability to meet its targets; and quality could be ignored, since intermediate and final buyers had little if any choice among products and suppliers.

Some growth did occur in the number of local collectively owned enterprises in the 1970s. As noted earlier, this was often at the initiative of local cadres operating around the central directive and despite the denigration of such enterprises as nonsocialist. They were set up to meet local needs from local inputs; only slight consideration was given to such factors as technology of production, or the quality and variety of outputs. The managers of these enterprises were lifetime employees controlled by the local authorities; workers were paid on the basis of work points (like the peasants), and there were narrow limits on permissible wage differentials among the workers. Private enterprises at the local level were strictly forbidden as capitalist.

Although there was no open unemployment, labor was used very inefficiently. There was little, if any, relationship between the productivity and wage of a worker. Everyone was assigned to a job guaranteed for life, and received a wage regardless of the amount of work done. Under Mao, as part of the deliberate effort to get away from material incentives, wages were frozen for lengthy periods, bonuses were eliminated during the Cultural Revolution, and promotions were very unusual. Skilled workers were stockpiled and forbidden to transfer regardless of available work so that skills were wasted. The result was both low labor productivity and a very high degree of under-employment. As a legacy of those policies, it was estimated that in mid-1988, after a decade of reform, there were fifteen million surplus workers in state-owned industrial enterprises alone, and a total of twenty to thirty million surplus workers if collectively owned in-dustrial enterprises were included. An indication of both that sur-plus and the low productivity of labor is that workers in many fac-tories actually worked less than four hours in an official eight-hour work day.[8]

These problems were exacerbated during the Cultural Revolution with its ideological stress upon continuous revolution, greater in-come and status equality, and breakdown of specializations. Many of the older and experienced managers, party leaders, and government officials with long revolutionary backgrounds were persecuted and dismissed; intellectuals were considered dangerous and, it not physi-cally persecuted, were sent to the fields and factories to learn from the peasants and workers. Old skills were lost, quite apart from such spe-cialists being unable to keep up with developments in their fields. Colleges and universities were closed for long periods, and when they were reopened, criteria for admission and graduation were based not on academic qualifications and records but on class background. The intellectual content of college education too was on an elementary level, and contact with foreign scientific thought was forbidden. (One field that was exempted from that restriction was nuclear power and weaponry.) Not surprisingly, China's level of technology in most in-dustrial fields lagged well behind that of other countries, developed and developing. At the same time a decade's building of human re-sources was lost.

As a summing up to the economic problems faced by China in 1978 after the death of Mao and the end of the Cultural Revolution, I quote below from a book by Ma Hong, one of China's most distin-guished economists and president of the Chinese Academy of Social Sciences when he wrote it in 1983.[9] The book begins with a review of the industrial achievements of China's communist regime for 1949 to 1978, which is interesting both for itself and for its remarks about In-dia, which Ma Hong, unlike many Indians, classifies as a capitalist country.

> [China] has been transformed from an old semi-feudal and semi-colonial country into a new socialist one. . . . We have built an independent and fairly comprehensive industrial and economic system on the foundations of the poverty and back-wardness of old China. . . . In 1980 industrial fixed assets [were] . . . more than 26 times greater than in 1952. . . . [Exist-

ing] industries . . . have all made significant advances. Many
new industries . . . have developed. . . . In the vast expanse of
China's interior regions . . . where there was virtually no industry before 1949, new industrial bases have now been set up. . . .

China [from 1950 to 1979] has caught up and even surpassed
India in the production of various industrial products in which
China was behind, while in the case of products in which China
was originally ahead, China's lead . . . has grown even big-
ger. . . . One [of these countries, China] is socialist and the other
[India] capitalist. With China's obviously greater achievements
in its post-liberation period, we can clearly see the superiority of
the socialist system. The rate of industrial growth in new China
has also surpassed the rates in the economically developed countries [from 1949 to 1977].

After summarizing these achievements, Ma Hong proceeds to the
problems and difficulties of that same period: "However [although
China's economic growth rate has been quite high, its] economic development has been very unstable with sudden ups and downs and
major swings in direction. Economic results have been relatively
poor and have had a tendency to decline. Thus the growth in national
strength has been fairly slow and the people have not derived much in
terms of material benefits."

Annual growth rates for both agricultural and industrial production fluctuated widely from plan to plan during the 1949 to 1975
period. In industry, the return on fixed investments in state-owned
industrial enterprises declined by almost 50 percent from 1957 to
1976; both the costs of construction projects and the time period for
completing construction projects have become much greater since
the First Plan (1953–57). "The investment needed to increase national income by one yuan" more than doubled between the First
Plan and the Fourth Plan (1971–75). With that rise in the capi-
tal/output ratio, the growth rate of national income also declined
over that period. An even more striking indication of a serious problem was that from 1957 to 1978, money wages of workers and staff in
state-owned enterprises rose by only 1 percent, living costs rose by 14
percent, and real wages *fell* by almost 12 percent. For a Communist
state dedicated to the welfare of the workers this failure to improve
workers' welfare raised not only economic issues but also potential
political and ideological issues.[10]

In Ma Hong's words, these results reflected "serious mistakes in
selecting the strategy and goals of our economic development and the
methods to achieve these goals." With respect to goals, "although we
often spoke of the aim of socialist production as being the satisfaction
of the people's needs, in reality we did not carry this out. . . . There

was instead a certain tendency to carry out production for the sake of production and an impatience for quick results, so that we often neglected economic and natural laws."

Ma Hong notes the following serious mistakes in the methods adopted to reach the industrial goals:

1. Emphasis on high targets in production and construction and neglect of economic results so that investment yields fell;

2. Overemphasis on "heavy industry at the expense of agriculture and light industry" in allocation of investments;

3. Overemphasis on new construction rather than "technical innovation and transformation of existing enterprises";

4. "[Overemphasis on] output of primary and intermediate products in such industries as iron and steel and [neglect of] production of final consumer goods." The unsold inventory of steel products was almost equal to the annual output of steel products; the unsold inventory of mechanical and electrical products was about equal to six months output. Meanwhile the supply of consumer goods, including consumer durables, was far short of demand;

5. Overemphasis on investment at the expense of consumption after the 1950s, so that "people's consumption levels relatively declined";

6. "[The closing of] the country to international contacts due to . . . narrow interpretation of the theory of self-reliance, resulting in waste which could have been avoided";

7. Elimination of individual ownership too rapidly by "unrealistically" stepping up the transfer to public ownership.

The number of self-employed workers in cities and towns fell from 8.8 million in 1952 to 1.0 million in 1957 to only 240,000 in 1975. "An over centralized system of economic management was also carried out within the sector owned by the whole people." As a result of these mistakes, Ma Hong concluded that "an unsound economic cycle of 'high speed, high accumulation, low efficiency and low consumption' was formed."

The 1984 decision of the central committee of the Communist party on the reform of the urban economic structure began by summarizing the major problems arising from those mistakes and indicating policy implications.

[The] rigid economic structure . . . cannot meet the needs of the growing forces of production. [There is] . . . no clear distinction . . . between the functions of government and those of enterprise; barriers exist between different departments or regions; the state has exercised excessive and rigid control over enterprises; no adequate importance has been given to commodity production, the law of value, and the regulatory role of the market; and there is absolute equalitarianism in distribution. . . . [Enterprises lack] necessary decision making power and the practice of "eating from the same big pot" [prevails] in the relations of the enterprises to the state and in those of the workers . . . to their enterprises. . . . [As] a result . . . the socialist economy is bereft of much of the vitality it should possess. . . . [We] tried to delegate power to local levels. . . . But this was limited solely to readjusting the administrative power of the central and local authorities and of the different departments and regions. The critical issue of giving enterprises decision-making power was not dealt with.[11]

The readjustment policies of the early 1980s followed by the outright reform policies after 1984, which will be presented in the next chapter, sought to address these problems.

INDIA

In the previous chapter I briefly outlined the goals of the Indian political leaders at independence with respect to economic development and industrialization and some of the plans for achieving these goals. In effect, by the early 1980s, the Indian government had created by its policies since 1950 a three-tiered industrial structure: the public sector, the large-scale and medium-sized private sector, and an extensive small-scale sector.

As a result of massive investment in the public-sector industry there was an increase from only five central-government-owned plants in 1952 to 223 such plants in 1983. In 1983 approximately two-thirds of the value of all capital assets in manufacturing was in the public sector. These government-owned plants produced 30 percent of value added in total manufacturing and over 40 percent in the factory sector of industry.[12] Private, foreign-controlled firms which had produced about one-fourth of India's manufacturing value added at independence had declined relatively, and were producing about 10 percent of output by 1984–85. The large-scale private Indian firms, which came under the antimonopoly laws, saw their share declining from about one-third of manufacturing value added to approximately 15 percent by the mid-1980s, while the medium-sized and small-scale sector produced almost one half of total manufacturing output, but only about a quarter of factory-sector output. Much of the output of the public-sector plants was in the production of capital and basic goods (the former includes machinery; the latter such products as fertilizers and heavy chemicals, cement, iron and steel, and nonferrous metals). The larger private firms which came under the licensing and other control procedures of the central government were largely concentrated in the production of intermediate goods (noncapital and basic inputs) and final consumer goods.[13]

The small-scale sector, which has been free of the licensing procedures, grew rapidly, although some of this growth has not been caught by the statistics. Apart from freedom from licensing, this sector, defined either in terms of value of capital or number of employees, depending upon the purpose, received tax and credit concessions, was free from the provisions of various worker protection laws, and perhaps most important after the mid-1970s, has reserved to it the production of over 800 manufactured products.

Domestically, enterprises in each of the three tiers were largely free from competition from firms in the other two tiers, or, except in the small-scale sector, by new or growing firms. Many of the capital and basic goods could be produced only in the public sector or by large private firms that had been producing those products in the 1950s, but whose expansion was forbidden or very tightly controlled. In all cases, the already existing larger private firms came under the government's licensing provisions and required a lengthy process of permission to expand or enter into new areas of production; new firms above a certain size also required permissions; small enterprises which did not need permission to start up could not grow above a certain size without losing their concessions and, more important, their reservation privileges. There were also price controls for one purpose or another, and for the textile industry, special controls on modernization and expansion of the factories to protect the handloom operations. In addition there were strict controls and permissions on foreign investment and tight limits on the importation of goods already produced in India, so that competition from outside India was also negligible.

The results of this industrial policy regime were mixed. On the one hand by 1980 India had a far larger industrial sector than it had in 1950, with a total output of manufactured goods over five times what it had been earlier. The compound rate of growth of industrial output at 6 percent per annum was about three times the preindependence rate, and was higher than the overall growth rate of gross domestic product. The share of manufacturing output as a percentage of GDP had risen from 10 percent in 1950 to 15 percent in 1983, but the share of total employment in industry (including manufacturing) had risen even less, from 11 percent in 1960 to 13 percent in 1981.[14] There had also been a great dispersion in the types of goods produced. Whereas in the early 1950s consumer goods production, largely textiles, dominated manufacturing, by the late 1970s such production had fallen to one-third of industrial output, with basic and capital goods production rising form 30 percent of the total to about 50 percent. India had a "wide spread of modern industries making everything from nuclear reactors to textile machinery, from machine tools to petrochemical plant."[15] The Narasimhan Committee remarked in 1985 that "dependence on imports in critical sectors has been substantially reduced [so that] . . . the proportion of imported machinery and transport equipment to gross domestic fixed capital formation in machinery and equipment has come down from about 40 percent in the fifties to less than 15 percent now."[16] Thus India's independence of foreign countries in terms of imports would also seem to have increased, thereby making apparent progress toward another of the goals of its industrial policy.

But despite these achievements there was, by the early 1980s, recognition within India of serious problems of "structural retrogression and stagnation in the industrial sphere."[17] The rate of growth in value added from industry fell from an annual average of 7 percent during the 1956–66 period to 5 percent from 1966 to 1982. There was also evidence of a significant rise in the capital/output ratios for the manufacturing sector, indicating declining efficiency in use of scarce capital resources.

The public sector, functioning within its own protected niche and with such social responsibilities as the development of regionally backward areas, earned, except for the petroleum refining sector, a negligible rate of return on its investment. K. S. Krishnaswamy pointed out that the public sector had not generated resources for further public investment, not only because of its social responsibility, but because of its weak management, its low productivity of workers protected by strong trade unions from discipline, and its reluctance to introduce new technology because of its possible impact on employment.[18] L. K. Jha goes on to note that the formal and informal controls and limits upon public-sector enterprises were more restrictive in fact than those for the private sector:

> Apart from the statutory controls which were applicable [to both sectors] the public sector was subjected to additional controls. . . . The expenditure of foreign exchange by the public sector enterprises was subjected to far greater scrutiny by government departments, than was the case with the private sector. . . . [In] the matter of pricing and distribution and even in respect of what it produced, the public sector was subjected to far greater control than the private sector. Even the appointment and salaries of its senior staff [and construction of their living quarters] needed the clearance of various government depart-

ments. . . . Management in the public sector . . . has also to comply with formal and informal directives given by the ministry under which an enterprise is located. . . . [Ministers] have to answer in Parliament about the detailed working of various enterprises and not just about their performance. There is . . . a tendency for the management of most enterprises not to take decisions on their own without consulting the Ministry, because of the fear of . . . [Parliamentary] criticism.[19]

The net effect of these controls and fears was that public-sector enterprises had little of the autonomy that they were expected to have under the 1956 Industrial Policy Resolution. The results in the public sector have been long delays in decision making, all too often very weak management, inability to reduce labor costs, and a frequent high-cost, low-return operation. In addition, while originally government ownership was meant for capital goods and basic industries, public ownership has served as a last resort for maintaining formerly private firms that would have otherwise gone bankrupt and closed, adding to local unemployment. The public sector thus has extended into production of many types of consumer goods as well as capital and basic products.[20]

As far as the large- and medium-scale private-sector firms subject to licensing and other restrictions are concerned, there was strong evidence as of 1969 that the licensing system had not fulfilled its goals of ensuring development of industry in line with plan priorities, preventing growth in nonessential industries, developing economically backward areas, or containing the concentration of economic powers. This awareness led to further legislation tightening controls on monopoly and foreign firms, but the effects of this were also not in line with its goals, and may have actually contributed to the decline in industrial growth rates in the 1970s. Apart from these results, "the restrictions and controls on private enterprise led to a very large degree of discretionary powers vested in the bureaucratic officers and their political masters which in turn led to bribery and corruption. The same restrictions also prevented technological updatedness and rise in productive efficiency with the result that Indian industry was internationally non-competitive. . . . The large measure of industrial development and diversification [that had occurred had not been] accompanied by a reduction in costs or increase in productive efficiency or technological updatedness. . . . Economies of scale could not be obtained because of restrictions on capacity, and since imports were strictly controlled, Indian industry obtained a sheltered market and failed to expand with the growing needs of a developing economy."[21]

While the role of small-scale enterprises had grown in the private

industrial landscape over the past thirty years, the reservation policies for a large number of commodities had negative effects in terms
of costs, technology, and quality of products. Economies of scale were
forgone for many products; since there was no competition from
larger firms in producing those reserved products there was little
pressure on small-scale firms to improve quality or develop technologically. While the freedom from licensing controls, the access to
credit, the tax exemptions, and the exemptions from labor legislation
encouraged the proliferation of small-scale firms, many of which are
believed to have been financed by larger enterprises because of those
exemptions, the costs arising from loss of these advantages might
well have discouraged their expansion and technological upgrading.
Instead expansion often took the form of a separate duplication of the
original small enterprise, under a nominally separate owner, with
both the original and new enterprise within the legal size limits. By
the early 1980s there were over one million small-scale enterprises,
employing approximately nine million workers and producing almost half of India's industrial output. The character of that development, however, reflecting the policy framework within which it
occurred, also contributed to the high cost of the output and the technological backwardness of the industrial sector.[22]

In such a protected and noncompetitive environment industrial
enterprises had little incentive for improved performance or greater
efficiency. Loss-making public-sector firms would be subsidized either by the budget or the banking system or by increases in fixed
prices that they charged customers. Both they and larger private firms
could operate at relatively low rates of capacity at which they made
acceptable profits at the prices charged. Small-scale firms might lose
their concessions if they grew too rapidly. In all three sectors quality
was of secondary importance. There was also little incentive to export. Profits were significantly higher in the domestic market; exports for many firms were simply a residual arising from some
temporary falling off of internal demand.[23] Not surprisingly the Indian government's *Economic Survey* for 1984–85 in its discussion of
industry ends thus:

> [Our] industrial performance has been unsatisfactory and a large
> area of industrial sector has been facing chronic structural prob-
> lems.
>   The disappointing performance of Indian industry is not
> limited to the Sixth Plan [1980–85] period. It was also a feature
> of the preceding fifteen years. . . . A number of factors have com-
> bined to result in the low productivity of resources in industry,
> including protection in various forms, inappropriate choices of

scale and technology, poor rates of capacity utilisation, mismatches between capacity and demand, and recurrent episodes of severe infrastructural constraints, especially with respect to power.

[If] the economy is to enjoy sustained growth at annual rates of 5 percent or higher, then the long-term growth of industry must accelerate to 8 or 9 percent a year. . . . The efficiency of industrial enterprises will have to improve markedly. The framework of industrial policy may also require changes but such reforms will only yield expected results if industry responds.[24]

Apart from the efficiency argument for change in the industrial policy system, there was also a connection between the licensing and control system and the increasing corruption in politics. I. G. Patel, former governor of the Reserve Bank of India, points out that "there was nothing particularly socialistic or egalitarian about the . . . license-permit-subsidy Raj which . . . helped to protect the turf of powerful vested interests and heaped on them the additional reward of much unearned rent as recompense for political and financial support. . . . Emphasis on integrity as distinct from efficiency will receive . . . widespread political support because the Indian psyche is still predominantly guided by moral rather than economic considerations. There is . . . need to emphasize the link between integrity in public life and economic efficiency."[25]

In Indian thinking industrialization was also regarded as the major instrument to raise India's living standards and reduce poverty. While industry had grown and living standards had improved, the reduction in poverty had been less than hoped for or promised since 1971. The political implications of this have been drawn by two of India's leading economists. C. T. Kurien remarks that "attending to the limited needs of the . . . [poorest groups in society] is essentially a political imperative of a socio-economic system whose policy is based on the principle of universal adult franchise. Elections . . . are held once in five years, or more frequently if . . . necessary. On these . . . occasions all political parties . . . become aware of the power of the masses and . . . that sovereignty vests with them. Promises are made to them and it is important . . . that these promises are kept at least as tokens."[26] V. K. R. V. Rao speaks of "the danger involved in not bringing the employment of the poor and . . . raising the income of the poor within the framework of the basic planning process." He goes on to warn of a potentially "explosive situation with] . . . *thunder in the air.*"[27] By the early 1980s there was a widespread realization that the industrial policy system was no longer working satisfactorily in terms of reducing poverty and raising general well-being. The political imperative of meeting the expected demands for improvement on the part of the large numbers of Indians who had benefited least from the economic changes since independence contributed initially to modest steps toward reform of industrial policy to raise rates of industrial growth taken under Indira Gandhi in the early 1980s, and then to their acceleration by Rajiv Gandhi in 1985.[28]

CONTRASTS IN PREREFORM
INDUSTRIAL PROBLEMS

A significant difference in the Chinese and Indian industrial systems before 1980 was that China essentially had a centrally planned and centrally controlled government or collectively owned industrial system. It was modeled on the Soviet system with respect to large-scale industry, although with a greater role for smaller enterprise and for local initiative and control than in the USSR. Trade too, whether domestic or foreign, was largely carried out by government agencies. A significant difference from the Soviet system was that in China wages were equal for the various classes of workers, and were based largely on seniority. Investment centered on heavy industry; consumer goods and agriculture were neglected and discriminated against. However the agricultural commune system contributed both to massive in-kind investments in rural irrigation and roads, to a relatively high level of education and health facilities in the rural areas, and to relative income equality within each rural area. Farm output however grew at only a low rate, roughly equal to population growth. The low rate of industrial and economic growth before 1978, combined with massive inefficiencies in the use of scarce capital resources, contributed to both lagging industrial technology, which threatened China's world political position, and stagnant living conditions, which undermined internal popular support for the Communist party. These pressures, within the context of the excesses of the Cultural Revolution, led directly to the shift in economic policy to stress economic growth, after Mao died in 1977.

India had not adopted the Soviet model of economic control and planning although there was stress on heavy industry. In fact, after Nehru's death, economic planning served more as an exercise than as a strong guide to policy. India, unlike China, had a large private industrial sector and encouraged private small-scale enterprises by various policies. Indian socialism, however, like China's, supported a greatly enlarged public sector by public investment; and this was combined with a tight system of control over the large private sector. The result was overall government control of industry, operating, however, through regulations rather than central plans and directives. As in China, priority was given to heavy-industry investment, largely in the public sector. Too, consumer goods were neglected and central investment for agriculture had low priority. Indian industry also functioned in a protected, noncompetitive market; and by the late 1960s the industrial growth rate had declined significantly compared to the previous period. Incentives to introduce new technology were weak in the protected internal market, and the regulations inhibited investment in new technology (this despite India's large technically trained population, unlike China). The Green Revolution had provided an earlier stimulus to rural demand for industrial products, but the effects were limited in space and over time as a result of the low public investment in agriculture.

As in China, the weakening industrial performance in the technological field threatened India's ability to maintain a strong international presence in the world and region. The slow industrial growth also undermined hopes for improved welfare for the great bulk of the population, while even the better-off had to resort to the black market to buy scarce consumer durables and better quality products. The complex regulatory system also contributed to a relatively high level of black-marketing and corruption from the interface between economics and politics. These factors contributed to a strong political demand for improved economic performance, especially in the field of industry, and for some reforms in the system that would contribute to both improved performance and a wider spread of the resulting benefits from that performance.

CHAPTER THREE

The Reforms

Even at the highest levels of the [Congress] Party, there has been unwillingness to think through policies to their logical implications
and to work out a strategy and programme appropriate to each case.
K. N. RAJ, "Hastening Slowly," 1959

CHINA

ON the death of Mao and the imprisonment of the "Gang of
Four," the new leadership was convinced that to renew the
credibility of the Communist party within the country and
to provide evidence of greater economic well-being for the people, as
well as to maintain China's leadership position in the world, economic growth and modernization were of high priority. There was
disagreement, however, as to the relationship between need for
growth and past events and ideology, and with respect to the pace of
change and priorities in the process of change.

Hua Guofeng, the new party leader and premier selected by Mao
himself as his successor, had been a provincial leader promoted by
Mao during the Cultural Revolution to his position as provincial
leader of Mao's own province, and then national leader. To insure his
rule he had overthrown the "Gang of Four," but he attempted to combine a loyalty to Mao's ideas, "the two whatevers," with a set of economic policies that aimed to accelerate the economic growth and
restore the economic system of the pre-Cultural Revolution. In 1978
he introduced the New Leap Forward, a ten-year plan to achieve a
widespread mechanization of agricultural production and a rapid development of industry, especially production of light consumer

This discussion of China's economic reforms has benefited greatly from my exchange of ideas with Mr. Buu Ruizhi.

goods. This called for a "massive super-industrialization, super-modernization programme" requiring both an increase in investment and "massive . . . imports of advanced technology and capital equipment from the West and Japan."[1]

Its implementation depended on a "spectacular development of China's petroleum [exporting] potential to earn the necessary foreign exchange." That massive program was criticized by Chen Yun, China's leading pre-Cultural Revolution economic policymaker, and his supporters, who argued that "haste makes waste." These critics "advocated balance over speed [and] consumption over accumulation" and were strongly critical of "production for the sake of production." A middle group, centering about Deng Xiaoping and his proposals of the 1970s, argued for the reform of China's economic and planning system in the longer run, and priority in the short run to renovating China's existing industrial plant to raise its ability to absorb new technology, before beginning a leap to modernize.[2]

In approximately one year Hua's Ten-Year Plan ended. While it yielded a high rate of growth, this was the result of one of the highest rates of investment (37 percent of national output in 1978) in China's post-1949 history, and a very rapid growth of imports not matched by exports, leading to China's largest trade deficit since the early 1950s. The higher money wages introduced by Hua, plus the very high investment level, the bottlenecks in construction, and the lagging increases in consumer goods supplies, led to what was then considered a serious threat of inflation and a large foreign exchange drain. (The cost-of-living index rose by almost 8 percent from 1979 to 1980 after an extended period of relative constancy and even decline in the previous decade. There was an annual trade deficit, which averaged 1.5 billion dollars from 1978 to 1980, after the near balance of the previous two decades.) The immediate policy consequence of the end of Hua's New Leap was a party statement advocating "readjustment, reform, consolidation and improvement of the current economic system" before beginning a program of "balanced development based on efficiency principles." This new policy was a victory of Hua's critics in the economic sphere and anticipated their subsequent political victory.[3]

Accompanying this shift in growth policy was a marked change in the party position on the role of ideology in relation to policy. While Hua supported Mao's later position on the primacy of ideology in governing policy, Deng and the reformers were successful in persuading the party to adopt the principle that "practice is the *sole* criterion of truth"—an earlier Maoist aphorism—in 1978. There was also a formal recognition that there were specialized areas of scientific knowledge in which professionally trained experts could offer objective and nonideological advice to the party and government. In July 1978, President Hu Qiaomu of the newly established Chinese Academy of Social Sciences spoke on "the objective nature of economic laws . . . 'independent of human will, consciousness and intention' . . . and the need to promote the science of economics" to provide guidance to policymakers.[4]

This was a sharp reversal of the dominant attitudes during the Cultural Revolution, when "economism" was attacked, economists were persecuted or sent to the fields, and economic and statistical institutions and agencies in and out of government were broken up. Economics was considered superfluous if not dangerous, since Mao and his supporters regarded the issue of "production relations" (i.e., the "class struggle") as *the* economic issue, while the issue of "productive forces" was considered irrelevant or ideologically threatening. "Production relations" was an ideological matter covered by Marxist-Maoist political economy, rather than an objective scientific study. Economics dealt with "productive forces," and was "concerned with economic efficiency, investment criteria, prices and growth theory." The Maoists considered China to be a "natural" rather than a "commodity" economy. Research on factors affecting the "productive forces" was both irrelevant and potentially dangerous in leading along paths that might be considered capitalist. Deng had been criticized as a "capitalist roader" for his remark "No matter whether the cat is black or white, if it catches mice it's a good cat"; he had been ousted from power in the mid-1970s when he proposed a program to strengthen the "productive forces" in China's commodity economy in order to accelerate economic growth.

The reacceptance of economics as an objective science reflected the victory of the reformers, both those seeking better balance and those seeking faster growth in the economy. Such matters as efficiency of resource use, the role of plan and market, the appropriate incentives to stimulate greater effort, and the use and structure of prices were of vital importance for the growth of a poor economy such as China. They were all matters on which economists, by using their discipline, might make an objective contribution.[5]

In one sector of the economy—agriculture—policy changes had already been initiated in 1978 even before they were formally permitted or adopted by the party. Decollectivization began in certain rural localities in Anhui and Sichuan provinces, and spread rapidly, contrary to official sanction. In December 1978 the party had ruled that all planning and farm management was to be carried out by teams; then in 1979 it forbade the division of land for family farming and the fixing of crop output quotas on a household basis. But in spite of these decrees, the household responsibility system had been adopted by most production teams in the country by early 1981. The State Agricultural Commission belatedly endorsed the new system at the end of that same year.

The changes in the agricultural responsibility system were followed by the reduction of state procurement quotas for grain, the liberalization of marketing, and the raising of prices for the quota share of output, combined with the freeing up of prices of the nonquota share sold in open markets. Now free.to take advantage of the massive investments in kind during the collectivization period, and stimulated by the price changes, the Chinese farmers greatly expanded their outputs. The gross value of output of the agriculture sector rose at an annual rate of 10 percent from 1979 to 1985. Within that average, commercial crop production apparently rose more rapidly than grain production, and production from sidelines (nonagricultural activities) grew even more rapidly than conventional agricultural production. The average per capita income of peasants was estimated to have increased by 90 percent over that same time period.[6]

That achievement led to a demand for industrial change and for greater output in the industrial sector also, to provide the industrial inputs and consumer goods that the peasants wanted with their higher incomes. The grass-roots localized experimental approach introducing the rural reforms provided a model for introducing changes in the urban sectors, while the contract system that was associated with the household responsibility system was seen as a potential instrument of reformed industrial management as well.

Another major direction of reform in rural areas that strongly influenced the growth of industry and commerce in those areas consisted of the decentralizing administrative and tax reforms that both gave local governments greater fiscal autonomy and made it more necessary for them to raise their own local tax revenues. "Overall the tax reforms have transformed local government officials from mere caretakers and administrators into *bureaucratic entrepreneurs* who take the lead in developing township and village industrial enterprises. . . . In contrast to the decollectivization in agricultural production and the withdrawal of local government from the day to day management of agricultural production, local officials intervene in almost every aspect of its [local industry] operation, from appointing the factory managers to determining the number of workers."[7]

There were also reforms in the management of these collectively owned local enterprises. They too, like the farm households under contract for agricultural output, were placed under a contract system.

They were run by managers appointed by the collective authorities and under contracts with the collectives. These appointments were for a fixed term, rather than for life, and the managers were responsible for meeting the terms of the contract, which included profitability goals. They were rewarded for overfulfillment of the terms of the contract by bonuses which could be high, and they could be dismissed if they did not meet those terms. Worker payment too was changed in the early 1980s from a work-point, hourly wage system to a piece-rate system with bonuses for good performance. The basic piece rates and bonuses were related to the enterprise's performance to motivate the workers further on behalf of their enterprise. Before 1978 most inputs to collective enterprises were supplied by state agencies at fixed prices, and most enterprise outputs were sold to state agencies at fixed prices. These restrictions were relaxed after 1978, earlier for the collectively owned enterprises than for the state enterprises. By the mid-1980s the collectively owned enterprises had far greater freedom to buy inputs, sell outputs, and set prices than did the larger state enterprises.

Another reform of the early 1980s allowed private nonagricultural enterprises at the rural level. These were permitted to hire workers, and while in theory there were limits on the number of workers they could hire, in practice some margin above those limits was permitted. A contributing factor to the rise of these private enterprises was the change in policy toward income differentials. In contrast to the strict limits on income differences before 1978, after 1978 the new slogan was "take the lead to get rich." Private entrepreneurship was encouraged and wide differentials in wages, bonuses, and income were allowed.[8]

While these reforms in the rural areas were taking place, major reforms were also introduced in the foreign-trade sector after 1978. Some policy changes to open China to trade had already begun to occur under Mao in the early 1970s, following the visit of President Richard Nixon to China. The volume of trade had increased and the direction of trade had widened, but foreign trade was still relatively minor in the economy. In 1979 the Communist party gave its official blessing to the open-door policy, with Hua's New Leap relying on foreign trade and imports of capital equipment from Japan and the West to achieve rapid modernization. Shortly thereafter serious theoretical discussion began on both the relevance of the theory of comparative advantage to China, and the ideological reconciliation of foreign trade within theoretical Marxism. But this was an area in which ideology played a subordinate role to practice. The new leadership had accepted the need for opening China to trade as part of the Four Modernizations program which had begun before Mao's death.

The main direction of foreign-trade reform before 1986 was to change the very centralized and rigid trading system, which put little pressure on the trading agencies to expand exports. Those agencies had previously operated under the Ministry of Foreign Trade, which had a monopoly over the import and export of all commodities, the targets of which were controlled by the plan directives. These reforms sought to give greater autonomy and responsibility to the trading units, to widen their decision-making powers, and to reward them for performance. The Chinese government took such measures as "decentralizing decision-making power to local authorities, industries and even production enterprises; merging trading corporations with production and commercial enterprises to negotiate and conduct trade; transforming trading corporations from administrative units for carrying out the directive of the superior bodies into independent economic entities with significant autonomy, and with material incentives to improve efficiency. Finally the scope of mandatory planning of foreign trade was greatly reduced while that of indicative planning was increased."[9] Today the Ministry of Foreign Trade monopolizes trade of only small groups of import and export products, rather than all trade, and it has lost its direct managerial authority over the trading companies. Instead the ministry has broader macro–policy-making powers over trade and some regulatory powers in the areas of foreign trade and economic relations. Too, after 1986 local governments and enterprises were allowed to retain 25 percent of the foreign exchange earnings from exporting goods; this retained foreign exchange is divided equally between the local government and the exporting enterprise.

But these reforms to encourage rural industry and to free foreign trade were only partly responsible for stimulating China's overall industrial growth and exports and for modernizing the economy. The key areas of the modernizing reforms would have to be in the urban sector.

Because such urban reforms were controversial, the first changes in the urban sector were specifically not considered reforms but rather "readjustments" of the Chinese economy following the overheating induced by the failed New Leap Forward. Chen Yun, who led the group arguing for the priority of readjustment, considered the dislocation of 1979 to be even more serious than that after the Great Leap Forward. There was need to cut down the "unrealistically high targets" of the past, "the excessively high rate of accumulation," the "blindly expanded scale of capital construction."[10] He called for a real emphasis on agriculture by higher investment there. In the industrial sector priority should be given to output of the light industry sector and consumer goods, rather than of heavy industry. Efforts to raise output from existing plants should be emphasized, as opposed to new construction. This called for both better management and the renovation of equipment and technology in existing plants. Rather than new industrial plants, the infrastructure fields of energy and transport should be given priority; and there was an urgent need for the development of science and education. Chen Yun emphasized the importance of proportionate development of the economy, in order to achieve appropriate balances in the demand for and supply of internal funds, foreign exchange, and materials. He felt that only with such an overall balance would high growth rates be possible. After 1980 the central government did order direct cuts in construction, internal finance, foreign trade, and investment to achieve the functional balances and production shifts that Chen Yun favored. They succeeded in cooling down the economy after the New Leap: the annual rate of price increase fell to 2 percent from 1981 to 1983; the foreign-trade deficits turned into surpluses after 1981. Also, comparing 1978 to 1984, the latter year saw the share of agriculture and light industry increasing as a percentage of the total output of agriculture and industry, and of light industry increasing in total industrial output. There was also a decline in the share of accumulation relative to consumption, although accumulation still remained at over 30 percent of the total output.[11]

While readjustment was given immediate priority after 1978, efforts were also started to increase output and raise efficiency of existing enterprises by reorganization of those enterprises. These steps were very carefully described as introducing the policies that Deng Xiaoping had advocated in the 1970s, and not as reforms. In the 1979–81 period these centered on measures to clarify the responsibilities of managers and others in the plant, to reduce financial losses, and to improve the quality of goods. They were also in line with Chen Yun's priorities; in Zhao Ziyang's ten principles for "readjusting, restructuring, consolidating and improving the national economy," presented in late 1981 to the National Peoples' Congress, readjustment and reorganization along the above lines were given higher priority than economic reform, which was simply listed as the eighth of the ten principles.[12]

More important in fact for the longer-run future of the reforms was the beginning of experiments in the direction of management reform in state-owned enterprises, first in 1978 in six firms in Sichuan province, where Zhao Ziyang was then party leader. These were extended to 100 firms in the same province in early 1979, and then to other provinces. The State Council, by a series of documents starting in mid-1979, formally authorized experiments in provinces and cities with respect to management decision making, profit retention, and taxation of and provision of credit to state-owned enterprises.

In these State Council–approved experiments of the late 1970s and thereafter, the purpose was to develop methods to motivate state-owned enterprises to behave like profit-seeking firms. One experimental direction was to permit these enterprises to retain a portion of their profits for their own use to establish separate funds for production improvement, for expanded welfare, and for rewards for exemplary performance. The second major direction was to allow these enterprises to produce output in excess of their plans if inputs were available, and to sell this excess output to nongovernment agencies; also, if they had excess capacity, they could use it to produce inputs for sale to other firms. Control over some of their own profits and excess capacity was limited and hedged by constraints, but these were tentative first steps to give enterprises a greater independence in their production and trading decisions. The provisions on profit sharing were complex and resulted in lengthy bargaining over shares between government and enterprises, and there was criticism over the fairness of the system because efficiency and profitability were only marginally related. In 1983, these difficulties led to the replacement of the profit-sharing system by a far less complex system of taxation of state-owned enterprises.

On the control and marketing side, in 1981 the government distinguished among three types of regulatory systems—mandatory planning, directive or guidance planning, and the market system—in determining a firm's production and sales. Certain key products, and the firms producing those, came under mandatory planning and a larger number under guidance planning. But there were also various stipulated conditions which allowed firms to buy and sell produce outside the formal channels, at prices which they could, within limits, set or negotiate.

A major political constraint on the freedom to set prices was the fear of rapidly rising prices which, in part, went back to the great inflation in the late 1940s that the Communist party succeeded in controlling. It was recognized that inflation would affect important segments of the Chinese population and their continued support of the government. The fast response to the relatively moderate price rise of 1981 reflected that worry, and prices remained under continued control during this readjustment period. Most prices were set by the government and were categorized as "list" prices. There was a smaller category of "negotiated" prices, i.e., prices "negotiated between the buyer and seller," that could fluctuate. "But only . . . nonessential or secondary [goods], or farm products in excess of the state purchase quota, fall in this category." Furthermore, these negotiated prices could fluctuate only within approved and relatively narrow limits. In the words of the director of the National Price Bureau:

> [Maintaining] price stability has been a consistent state policy . . . since 1949. It is true that for complex and historical reasons, the present pricing system has many irrational elements. . . . [These are] definitely detrimental to the planned, proportionate development of the national economy. . . . However the actual adjustment of prices will be a very complex process, as it entails a redistribution of interests among the various regions and economic departments.
>
> The present pricing system will be adjusted very slowly and step by step, as production develops and the national economic strength grows. This will take five years at least. In the meantime the policy of maintaining a basic stability of prices will be strictly adhered to.[13]

One continuing element in readjustment, on which there was a broad spectrum of agreement, was the Open Door policy, which went back to Mao. Annual trade levels from 1973 to 1977 doubled in value compared to the previous decade, but imports and exports remained in approximate balance. There had been massive increases in trade values and in deficits during Hua's New Leap Forward from 1978 to 1980, but with tightening thereafter, a balance had once again been restored in 1980–83. During this period the Open Door was recognized over a wide spectrum of Chinese opinion as necessary if China was to modernize; the worry was more over the deficit and its possible implications for China's economic independence.[14]

With excellent crops in 1984, food was available in abundance and prices had stabilized. The Chinese economic situation had apparently improved sufficiently following the rural reforms and urban readjustment for the government to place urban economic reform at the top of its agenda. This was set forth in a decision of the party's central committee in October 1984.

> Our successes in rural reform and the demands on the cities by the growing rural economy provide highly favorable conditions for restructuring China's entire national economy, focusing on the urban economy. . . . Political unity and stability are ever more consolidated; major successes have been achieved in economic readjustment; the economy has been growing

steadily; the major targets of the Sixth Five Year Plan (1981–85) have been fulfilled ahead of schedule; and the country's financial situation has improved gradually. . . . [The] sound all-round consolidation of party organizations at [all levels] has set . . . to rights the ideas guiding all fields of work in modernization, and has given . . . the reform a clear orientation. Conditions are now ripe for all-round reform of the economic structure. . . . [The essential purpose of the reform is to] "develop the forces of production [and] create ever more social wealth [within the socialist system]. . . . We must . . . concentrate on economic development and modernize China's industry, agriculture, national defence and science and technology.[15]

For such development the urban enterprises are crucial; the purpose of reform is to revitalize these enterprises, especially the large and medium-sized ones. Revitalization requires steps to increase the decision-making power of the enterprise.

On the premise of following the state plan . . . the enterprise should be truly made . . . independent and responsible for its own profit and loss and capable of transforming and developing itself. . . . Modern enterprise [too] calls for centralized and unified leadership and direction of production and strict labour discipline. . . . Under socialism, there is unity between the authority of the enterprise's leadership and the status of the working people as masters of their initiative and creativity. . . .
Correct relations between the state and the enterprise and between an enterprise and its workers and staff are the essence . . . of the restructuring of the national economy. . . . [This] inevitably calls for reform of every aspect of the entire economic structure. This involves a whole range of reforms including planning, pricing, economic management by state institutions, and the labour and wage system. . . . [They] should basically be accomplished in about five years.[16]

These generalizations were followed by a ten-point program increasing the decision-making powers of management of state-owned industrial enterprises with respect to their ability to: (1) control their own production after completing their planned production; (2) sell their output in the market, including a small amount of the planned output; (3) select their own suppliers of inputs; (4) control use of most of their own depreciation funds for investment and sell or rent out idle equipment, provided the revenues from such sales were used for investment; (5) determine their own internal organization and allocation of labor; when recruiting workers managers had the right to select the new workers; (6) raise wages of outstanding workers and staff, and this power could be used to reward 39 percent of the firm's labor force instead of 19 percent as before; and, (7) cooperate with other firms without any change in their control or financial system.

Related to these specific intra-enterprise reforms, which enhanced the power and responsibility of the management, was an administrative reform that increased the power of the city vis-à-vis the province or central government department in relation to both planning and control of enterprises. Cities were now able to prepare their own plans and get clearances directly from the national planning agency, thus bypassing many midlevel bureaucrats. At the same time, many urban enterprises were shifted from the control of the central government departments to that of the cities in which they were located, reducing the number of their clearances for planning purposes.

This key 1984 document also spoke more generally of the role of planning and the appropriate types of planning under which enterprises operate. It recognized the difficulty of comprehensive mandatory planning that would rely on administrative orders in a country such as China, and recognized the need to rely on "economic levers and the market" as well. But it added that China is "a planned commodity economy, not a market economy"; that there is a need for mandatory and guidance planning, and that "guidance plans are fulfilled mainly by the use of economic levers. . . . [M]andatory planning will be applied to major products . . . [and] major economic activities. Other products and . . . activities which are far more numerous should either come under guidance planning or . . . the operation of the market."[17]

The document went on to state that the law of value applies within a socialist planned economy, but that this had been neglected in China. That neglect "[contributes to] much confusion in our present system of pricing. The prices of many commodities reflect neither their value nor the relation of supply to demand. The irrational price system has to be reformed. Otherwise it will be impossible to assess correctly the performance of enterprises . . . and rationalize the production mix and consumption mix. . . . The various aspects of the reform in economic structure, including planning and wage systems, depend to a large extent on reform of the price system. . . . [Reform] of the price system is the key to reform of the entire economic structure. . . . As the reform of the price system affects every household . . . we must be extremely prudent . . . we must adopt effective measures to ensure that the real income of [all] inhabitants does not go down as a result of price readjustments."[18]

Unfortunately for the actual introduction of price reform, there was another inflationary trend in late 1984 and 1985. In 1984, the cost-of-living index of staff and workers rose by almost 3 percent and in 1985 it rose by another 12 percent.[19] This latter was a higher rate of increase of this index than in 1979–80 and the highest since 1961. General price reform that might lead to still higher price increases was clearly not in the cards.

Despite this there were two significant directions of reform in the price area. One was a further freeing of the marketing and pricing of farm products after the record 1984 crop; the second was the placing of the prices of heavy industry products on a two-track basis. The planned output was to be sold at a government set price; output beyond the plan could be sold at the market price. This was expected to be a transition step toward the goal of market pricing for most goods. At the time of adopting the two-track policy, market prices of such basic industrial goods were far higher than the fixed prices, and a general freeing up would raise prices significantly. It was hoped that as output rose over time the difference between fixed and market prices would diminish: market prices would fall and the fixed prices would be raised to cover costs. In fact this convergence did not happen; rather a dual price system continued, with a connection between each set of prices taking the form of illegal shifts of price-fixed goods, often greased by bribes, from the controlled market to the higher-priced free market.

Efforts, meanwhile, were continued to give the enterprises greater independence and to increase the power of the managers and the productivity of the workers to raise profitability of the firms. Experiments were permitted in the leasing of plants to managers of collective and smaller state-owned firms, and in introducing a capital management responsibility system to stimulate managers to increase the capital assets of their plants. Various documents were also issued by the State Council to clarify the rights of managers in the employment of workers and the division of responsibility between managers and party secretaries. Managers who met their annual targets were permitted to earn two to three times the average wage of workers in their plants, and outstanding managers could earn even more. However those who failed to meet their targets could have their salaries reduced. These experiments were formalized by the introduction of the Management Responsibility System, which, in effect, contracted out the management of state-owned enterprises. Under this system ownership of the enterprises was separated from managerial authority. Managers were appointed on a contract of three to five years; those contracts specified their targets of performance for overall profit and the government's share of profit, and for technology improvement. They also made clear the managers' rewards and penalties for meeting or not meeting those targets. By 1988, managers of about 80 percent of the large and medium-sized enterprises in China were under this system.

In October 1987, Zhao Ziyang, then the formal leader of the Communist party of China, presented his report to the Thirteenth Party Congress. In this he strongly advocated the acceleration of the reform program to "[invigorate] enterprises . . . by separating ownership from managerial authority" by such means as the contract system, leasing, and share ownership; "[promote] horizontal ties between enterprises" and break down barriers between them; establish and improve the "socialist market system," by extending it to factors of production; improve the macroeconomic control system so that it becomes the major means for the state to apply "economic levers in an all around way," with direct state control being limited in time and extent; encourage other types of ownership—"cooperative, individual and private"—than just public, although public ownership would remain the "predominant" form; encourage distribution of wages according to work by such means as piecework; and permit forms of income other than wages to such social groups as private owners, risk-takers, and shareholders. That report also represented the philosophy of the entire reform effort.[20]

The centerpiece of the industrial reform effort has been to reduce gradually the scope of mandatory planning "by such means as signing contracts . . . by which the state places orders for goods with enterprises, and enterprises with one another. The state should gradually shift to using mainly indirect means to control enterprises. . . . [In turn, we must] change the managerial mechanisms of enterprises. . . . In general it is not appropriate for the state to take direct control over [government-owned enterprises], or their vitality will be stifled. . . . It is . . . essential to separate ownership [i.e., the state] from managerial authority, to give enterprises real power of management . . . so that they [enterprises] are able to make their own management decisions and take full responsibility for their own profits and losses." This calls for the use of contracts between the state and enterprise managers to define "their respective responsibilities, powers and interests"; the selection of qualified managers through competition, and their reward or penalty on the basis of their performance; "a system under which directors or managers assume full responsibility, . . . tighten labour discipline and enforce strict scientific management of production. . . . We must adhere to the principle that distribution according to work remains predominant. . . . [We should] encourage some individuals to become prosperous before others through good management and honest work. . . . Where possible, we should introduce piece-rate wages and wages based on work quotas maintaining strict control over product quality and work quotas. . . . We should . . . promote [horizontal economic ties and] groups and associations [among enterprises] in our effort to deepen the reform. . . . We should resolutely reject the concept of a self-enclosed natural economy and change the backward state of affairs in which an enterprise, whether big or small, is a self-contained unit."[21]

Related to these enterprise reform actions were a whole series of other steps: the strengthening of cities to become "multi-functional economic centers" by streamlining administration and delegating more powers to local levels; reforming the pricing system by "rationalizing the prices of commodities and of the essential factors of production . . . [with] the state [setting] the prices of a few vital commodities and services, while leaving the rest to be regulated by the market." There was also room for a private sector, a "necessary and useful supplement to the public sector," as was a foreign-investment sector.

Such reforms too called for the development of an effective macrocontrol system "with a view to keeping a basic balance between society's total supply and total demand . . . [and ensuring] a reasonable apportionment of revenues between the central authorities and local authorities."

The economic reforms were in turn associated with reforms in the relations of the Communist party and its organizations to the government itself and to enterprises. At the enterprise level "Party organizations . . . , instead of attempting to provide centralized leadership . . . should support the directors and managers in their assumption of overall leadership." These changes in the role of the party were to be accompanied by changes in the relationship of the central to the local authorities in making and carrying out policies. "[It] is essential to . . . distinguish between the duties of [central authorities and local authorities to ensure that] local matters will be handled by local authorities, while the central authorities determine major policies and exercise supervision. [But regardless of the level of government in] relations between government and enterprises . . . powers of operation and management [are to be delegated to the enterprises] . . . [while] the government is to provide services for enterprises and the supervise them in accordance with laws, regulations and policies."[22]

Shortly thereafter, an Enterprise Reform Law defining the relations between an enterprise and the government and party was passed, as well as a Bankruptcy Law setting forth the conditions under which a firm could be declared bankrupt, but both were worded so loosely that their implementation was problematic.

In May and June of 1988, the party and government began to take steps to introduce broad price and wage reforms to end "irrational" price-setting. The first of these, in late May, was to raise the various nonstaple food prices in the cities by 30–60 percent and to give wage subsidies to urban workers to compensate.[23] Just before that action Deng remarked that "over the years China has had to allocate a large proportion of the annual state revenue in the form of food subsidies. . . . After the successful completion of the food price reform, China is looking forward to solving the raw material price problem. . . . The price and wage reforms . . . [are] critical to achieve the goal of developed-country status by 2050. . . . [The] reforms cannot be carried out piecemeal." In mid-June he added, "[They] must be tackled in a comprehensive way. . . . [Conditions] are ripe . . . to take the risk of all-round price and wage reforms."[24]

In the event, this price reform effort failed, in part because the price rises of 1987 and early 1988 had contributed to the unhappiness and fall in living standards of many urban residents. Li Peng, reporting to the Seventh National People's Congress in March 1989, stated that "instead of taking vigorous measures in good time to stabilize finance and control prices . . . we relaxed control over . . . the prices of more commodities, only to intensify the panic of the masses over the price hikes and evoke a buying spree . . . in many localities." The party leaders had decided in September 1988 to give stability a higher priority within the economic goals, focusing on "improvement and rectification." Consequently Li Peng's report argued that "we must tighten control over prices. . . . No departments, localities or enterprises shall be allowed to raise, without authorization, the prices of capital and consumer goods . . . under the control of the State Council. . . . Ceiling prices . . . for major farm and sideline products, industrial consumer goods and certain means of production must be adhered to. . . . [For] price rises for major commodities enterprises must apply to higher authorities for approval, and it is necessary to stop exploitation by middlemen and resale [from one place to another] at a higher price."[25] While the enterprise reform goals were also formally reaffirmed by Li Peng, in effect the economic reform process was put on hold, especially with respect to prices. This retreat reflects the fact that the political exigencies following the student demonstrations of 1986–87 and the price rises of 1988 had become of primary importance relative to economic issues.

INDIA

In India a low-key movement toward liberalizing reform began at a slow pace after Indira Gandhi returned to power in 1980 following the Janata government of the previous three years. Atul Kohli has remarked that some of the political motivation for Indira Gandhi's tentative relaxations of controls was to gain greater business support for her party.[26] Her expansion of reservations for small-scale industry was similarly motivated. There were also genuine economic issues: industrial growth had been lagging over the past decade; India was falling behind technologically in such rapidly developing fields as electronics; with rising incomes there was a demand for consumer durables such as television sets, which Indians visiting overseas found elsewhere, and for more and better automobiles, motorcycles, and other vehicles. An issue that had become of greater importance as nondevelopmental current government expenditures increased, was the need to raise resources for investment. This led to a closer examination of the generally weak financial performance of public-sector enterprises and their inability to generate investment resources. The steep oil price rise of 1979 contributed to a worsening of India's terms of trade and threatened further deterioration in its balance of payments; urgent action was needed to raise Indian exports and foreign exchange receipts. With such political and economic pressures there was a greater interest on the part of Indira Gandhi and her advisers in the backlog of previous expert committee reports which had recommended liberalizing reforms in various aspects of the control system. Mrs. Gandhi also established additional expert committees in the early 1980s to examine particular areas of the economic policy framework.

The Sixth Five-Year Plan of 1980, prepared by the new government after the early scrapping of the defeated Janata party's Fifth Plan, emphasized the need for greater industrial efficiency and improved industrial performance in general, as well as for technological upgrading; 1982 was declared to be "the year of productivity." Various steps were taken to modify aspects of the existing control system to reduce its rigidity. These included introducing a dual price system for cement to replace the previous set price on all cement output; raising somewhat the exemption limit for the licensing of new enterprises; allowing more automatic increases in industrial capacity in selected industries; freeing certain key industries from the provisions of the antimonopoly act with respect to additional permissions required by that act; initiating a new electronics policy in early 1984 to ease technology transfer from the West and to liberalize control over the computer industry; and allowing the private sector, within limits, to enter the manufacture of telecommunications equipment. Related to these steps was the adoption of a policy to raise output and widen the distribution of television sets in the country.

With respect to foreign economic relations there was significant liberalization of import of raw materials and components, and a lesser degree of liberalization of import of capital goods. The permissible range of industries open to investment by foreign companies under the Foreign Exchange Regulation Act of 1973 was enlarged in 1982 to encourage technology upgrading. Nonresident Indians were also extended special privileges permitting them to bypass controls on foreign investment and remission of foreign exchange, to encourage them to invest in Indian industry. In 1980–81, Mrs. Gandhi negotiated the largest loan—SDR 5 billion—made by the International Monetary Fund (IMF) to any country up to that date. While this was criticized within India by radical intellectuals, it provided a reserve for possible foreign exchange contingencies in the following years; it was repaid before its due date, in part for political reasons as a sign of success. While these might be called liberalizing steps, Indira Gandhi's government also took some backward steps with respect to expanding competition, most notably by increasing the number of products reserved for production in the small-scale enterprise sector from 500 to over 800.

The net positive effect of these industrial policy changes was however minor upon industrial growth and structural change. In fact, in the 1980–85 period, the annual industrial growth rate of 5.5 percent was below both the Sixth Plan target of 7.0 percent and the trend rate of 6.0 percent for the previous three decades. With respect to achievements of that period, the following Seventh Plan refers to various technological advances in the area of computer and electronic communication use in industry, but it points out that their impact on productivity was negligible, other than in the specific new projects in which they were actually used. Steady technological upgrading did not take place and the gap between India and the leading countries in technology remained large. In spite of a major policy statement and some consolidation of the infrastructure in science and technology, India's development in those fields remained low.[27]

Isher Ahluwalia summarized the economic results of this slow and early "liberalization" as tending "to be marginal. . . . [Some] of the measures . . . in fact amounted to a catching up with events. . . . [for example, the] increases in the exemption limit for industrial licensing . . . in 1982 have to be seen in the context of rising prices."[28]

Looking at the political impact, Kohli remarks that "Indira herself down played the significance of . . . economic achievements as tools of legitimacy. When attention did turn to the economy the picture for popular consumption was more of continuity than change. The rhetoric of socialism . . . was maintained. . . . The changes themselves appeared largely technical. . . . The attempt was made to depoliticize economic decisions as far as possible. . . . [Her] attempts to liberalize the economy did not draw sharp political reaction. . . . The tension between the pursuit of economic rationality and the rationality of democracy . . . was kept within manageable bounds. It is hard to know how far she intended to push liberalization."[29]

After Indira Gandhi's assassination in late 1984, and Rajiv Gandhi's succession and overwhelming election victory early in 1985, the speed of liberalization accelerated to a breathtaking pace. During the eighteen months after the election, "forty-six packages of liberalization in the areas of trade, taxation and industrial policies" were introduced.[30] Many of these specific policy changes resulted from "the . . . recommendations of a number of committees set up [earlier]. . . . The [policy] decisions thus represent a general consensus arrived at as a result of prolonged national experience of planning and the regulatory and control measures experimented with for this purpose. However, but for the new Prime Minister . . . the changes would have been slower, more protracted and less interconnected." But this was somewhat a conjecture since "there has been no systematic policy on the publication of these reports or the announcement of the decision on their recommendations. The decisions have . . . often been taken *ad hoc*."[31] Subsequently S. Guhan, one of India's distinguished economists with long experience in economic policy-making, also remarked on the "restructured and *ad hoc*" character of the liberalization process, reflected in the fact that "till now [1988] there has been no 'white paper' on liberalization."[32] Kohli, in presenting the political background for this speeding up of the pace of reform, argues that Rajiv Gandhi regarded his overwhelming political victory in January 1985 as a personal mandate, giving him the power to make the changes that he and his associates felt were necessary to bring India into the twenty-first century. There was also the sense that a new generation had come to power. Rajiv brought with him advisers who were contemporaries with similar technocratic and managerial interests and who had won, at least for a short time, the power to move the state to do what they thought was necessary to unleash India's economic energies. Although no white paper aiming at a broad political impact was issued, the Seventh Five-Year Plan, which appeared in late 1985 after some of the specific reforms had been introduced, puts these and other subsequent reforms into a broader context. Significantly, the vice-chairman of the Planning Commission was Dr. Manmohan Singh, previously governor of the Reserve Bank of India, a professional economist of Rajiv's generation, especially knowledgeable on India's foreign trade problems. Another key adviser on economic issues in Rajiv's secretariat was Montek Ahluwalia, also a professional economist of the newer generation.

The Seventh Five-Year Plan starts by placing the plan within a broader context of economic goals for India in the year 2000 (not dissimilar to China's longer-term framework and goals). These are "the elimination of poverty and creating conditions of near full employment, the satisfaction of the basic needs of the people in terms of food, clothing and shelter, . . . universal elementary education, and access to health facilities for all. It should be the aim to create . . . the conditions for self-sustaining growth in terms of both . . . finance . . . and the development of technology. In the sphere of industry efficiency must be . . . improved so as to attain international competitiveness in major products . . . Creation of opportunities for productive employment of a growing labor force assumes top priority. . . . [Around] 120 million persons will be added to the labour force over the next 15 years. . . . The most important structural change to be brought about in the [1985–2000] period will be the accelerated rate of growth of industry and its much greater relative contribution to national output and employment." Indian industry would have to grow at 8–9 percent per annum during this period. An efficient and flexible industrial structure was needed, to sustain India's exports, and meet the greater internal demands for industrial inputs by the agricultural sector, and for mass consumption of goods in general. This called for "reform of [the industrial] management system [and] . . . increased domestic competition" to create a climate "more conducive to growth, reduction of cost and improvement in quality." India must "keep abreast of the new technologies in the areas of electronics, biotechnology, robotics, and new materials. . . . The management of science and technology development will need to be reviewed. . . . Arrangements for access to technology need to be improved.[33]

An appropriate environment has to be created so as to encourage and promote greater efficiency, higher productivity and faster industrial growth . . . through a well coordinated system of incentives and in consonance with . . . self-reliance. Accelerated growth of manufacturing, accompanied by radical restructuring and induction of "sunrise" industries within a suitably modified policy frame would bring about a significant transformation of India's industrial economy.

To facilitate this process, industry will have to upgrade technology and management, attain economies of scale, pursue greater value-added activities and selectively launch an export drive. . . . State intervention will undergo a qualitative change that will emphasize its developmental role [and] greater interaction with industry and forge closer links between industry, trade and finance. . . . Apart from basic industries, the major thrust in . . . industrialization would be toward mass consumption goods and export industries."

Many of these industries were in the private sector but the plan envisaged a continued role for the public sector, especially in the high tech industries, in research and development, and by generating "sizable resources for investment."[34]

"[Policy] measures will be needed to promote an efficient industrial structure which lays emphasis on cost reduction, quality improvement and up gradation of technology. Structural reforms will be needed in the management of public enterprises so that these . . . can meet production targets and also generate adequate internal resources for their expansion."[35]

In the shorter five-year perspective, the Seventh Plan sought an industrial growth rate of 8 percent from 1985 to 1990; it also projected the start of the restructuring of industry toward "high technology, high-value-added and knowledge-based industries like electronics, advanced machine tools and telecommunications [and developing] . . . appropriate links . . . between defence needs and industry. The main objective of . . . restructuring would [be to] take India into the rank of leading industrial countries of the world. . . . [The] programs in the Seventh Plan will focus on the efficient use of [most industrial] investments so that surpluses could be generated. . . . This will apply especially to those units where capacity utilization has been low. . . . It is . . . essential that . . . health of the existing projects be fully ensured before any expansion is undertaken."[36]

The plan document went on to speak of a policy package to stimulate substantial competition within the industrial sector, using a system of incentives rather than fiat to direct growth in the desired new areas, as well as to encourage investment in modernization of such older industries as textiles. The aim would be to reduce costs of production and improve the quality of the output both to meet internal demand and to develop export possibilities. An important method of making the performance of the public sector "more dynamic" might be "to inject an element of competition within the public sector and in certain cases with the private sector. . . . Industrial Policy should . . . encourage involvement of the private sector for the development of 'sunrise' industries in high technology areas." There was a need to give management of public-sector enterprises greater autonomy, to weed out public-sector industrial units that had little hope for greater efficiency, and no longer to regard the public sector as the resting place for unviable private units. With respect to the private sector the plan remarked that "excessive regulation and persistence with outdated controls can be counterproductive." It pointed out that various committees had examined aspects of the system and recommended steps, "to liberalize and modify . . . policies and procedures."[37]

The expectation was that with government investment in infrastructure, liberalization of controls, incentive for development of "thrust" areas, and the new fiscal policy, greater enthusiasm and initiative would be generated among the private industrial entrepreneurs. In the electronics field, particularly, the basic thrust of policy was to be on general liberalization of licensing, greater reliance on fiscal incentives rather than physical controls, producing at the volumes of economic scale compatible with current technology, and attracting nonresident Indians to play a significant role in the development of the industry. As a subset of that specific development, emphasis was to be placed not only on producer goods, but also on greater production of electronic consumer durables such as televisions, as well as a wide range of other energy-using products, in which the private sector played a major role. One symbol of this relatively greater role for the private sector in the Seventh Plan was that private-sector investment was projected at somewhat over half of total planned investment—the first time since the First Five-Year Plan of the early 1950s that this had occurred.[38]

While the Seventh Plan document somewhat postdated the actual start of Rajiv Gandhi's accelerated reform program, the particular reforms with respect to industry, foreign trade, and taxation fit into that plan's broader framework. However, the reforms themselves were specifically patterned on the method used earlier, and much more cautiously, by Indira Gandhi—i.e., accepting the overall regulatory framework but modifying the existing controls and procedures to give enterprises greater leeway, by such methods as widening specific areas of exemption by sectors and/or raising size limits. Isher Ahluwalia indicates the overall character of these measures as taken "with a view to limiting the role of licensing, expanding the scope for contribution to growth by large houses, encouraging modernization, raising the investment limits for . . . the small sector . . . , and encouraging existing industrial undertakings in certain industries to achieve minimum economic levels of operations." She then lists the following specific "important measures":

(1) delicensing of a number of industries: some twenty-five broad categories of industries, e.g., electrical equipment, automotive ancillaries, machine tools, . . . and eighty-two bulk drugs and formulations were delicensed in March 1985, while roller flour mills and some chemical industries were later added to the list; delicensing was also extended to twenty-two of the twenty-seven MRTP [Monopolies and Restricted Trade Practices] industries exempt under sections 21 and 22 of the MRTP Act; (2) broad-banding of certain industries with a view to providing flexibility to manufacturing to produce a range of products: by January 1986, some twenty-eight industry groups, e.g., metallurgical machinery, earth-moving machinery, auto ancillaries, machine tools, were covered under this facility, and during 1986 the facility was extended to industries such as glass, steel pipes and tubes, synthetic fibers and synthetic filament yarn, electrical cables and wires, ball and roller bearings, specified categories of agricultural machinery, textile machinery and chemical industries; (3) expanding the role of large houses/enterprises by broadening the list of industries (now thirty-two industries) open to them . . . ; (4) raising the asset threshold to Rs 100 crores for MRTP houses, thereby enabling a larger number of companies to operate without the restrictions of the Act; (5) permitting MRTP companies in twenty-seven industries, e.g., machine tools, portland cement, machinery for chemical industries, certain types of electronic components and equipment, to directly seek a license without first obtaining prior and separate clearance from the Department of Company Affairs (exempting the MRTP companies in the twenty-seven industries from sections 21 and 22 of the Act); (6) raising of investment limits for the small-scale sector and providing fiscal incentives for the promotion of the small-scale sector; (7) exempting from licensing requirements increases up to 49 percent over licensed capacity for purposes of modernization/renovation/replacement; (8) announcing national policies relating to specific industries such as textiles, sugar, electronics and computers; (9) making it easier to import foreign technology for purposes of modernization and upgrading of quality; and (10) . . . instituting a scheme to encourage existing industrial undertakings in certain industries to achieve minimum economic levels of operations.[39]

Geeta Gouri rightly points out that these liberalization policies were "not a simple 'return to market forces' situation. Bureaucratic controls persist through the caveats attached to the policies." Many of the measures apply only if the plant is to be located—or is located—in a backward industrial area, if the product is not reserved for the small-scale sector, if the plant is not located within defined urban limits, if the industries are not polluting, and if their import requirements are below a certain size.[40]

These liberalization measures, too, were largely concentrated in the capital goods and basic metal sectors, for selected chemicals and drugs, and the paper industry, in all of which the enterprises tend to be in the public sector. In the telecommunications area the production of equipment, hitherto reserved for the public sector, was opened to the private sector. In India's oldest private industry, the textile industry, which faced many problems because of restrictions on modernization of the mills designed to protect small enterprises, limits on capacity were removed. In addition, the private sector was permitted to engage in such activities as road-building, hitherto limited to the public sector.

These steps in industrial production proper were accompanied by some liberalization of imports as a step toward upgrading India's industrial technology, raising the quality of Indian manufactured goods, reducing their costs of production and prices, and improving their competitive trade position. In particular, imports of capital goods which were not produced in India were eased by reducing the required permissions, formalities and customs duties for such imports by export-oriented enterprises. Steps were also taken to reduce licensing procedures for export-oriented enterprises and to allow both greater and speedier access to foreign exchange for imports of raw materials and components used in production of exports, and for their promotion overseas. Schemes were expanded to compensate exporters for tariffs paid on such imports, for excise duties on domestically produced inputs, and for above world prices for input for export-oriented output, as well as for promotion of exports, and the procedures by which exporters received such compensation were simplified and shortened. In addition, for the first time, the government announced a three-year import-export policy to provide some stability to foreign-trade policy.[41]

But despite these actions, as D. T. Lakdawala points out, the import liberalization that took place "is mainly to facilitate exports. So far as consumption goods are concerned, their imports are largely banned. . . . There is an effort in principle to replace quantitative controls by tariffs, but goods in bulk and other canalised goods [goods imported through government channels] account for half the imports. . . . Imports of capital goods are liberally allowed, but some of the duties . . . lowered in 1985–86 [were] . . . raised in 1986–87. [Except for electronics and communications] . . . there is no appreciable change . . . in imports of intermediates. [As before,] entry of foreign capital except non-resident [Indian] investment . . . to be welcome . . . must be accompanied with sophisticated technology. Collaboration is yet permitted only on a case-by-case basis, though . . . permissions are more readily given."[42]

Another area of reform was in the fiscal area to rationalize the existing tax system, increase revenues, and provide greater stability for policies. Both individual and company income tax rates and procedures were simplified to make tax computation and payment easier, and tax rates were reduced in order to encourage payment; at the same time enforcement of tax laws was made more stringent to raise the cost of nonpayment. Even more important, because it affects the indirect tax system which is the greater source of revenue, was the beginning of the rationalization of that system by the introduction of a Modified Value Added Tax (MODVAT). This provided for the reimbursement of excise taxes on inputs in the production of a large number of products in order to eliminate the price-cascading impact of these excise taxes. To stimulate export promotion by Indian firms in 1985 and 1986, taxes were more than halved on the profits earned from exports, and in 1988 those taxes were entirely eliminated. Many of these steps and directions were contained in the Long Term Fiscal Policy Statement of 1985, which sought to provide a previously lacking stability in tax policy for the next five years.

Apart from increasing revenue, it was hoped that the tax reforms would lead to a greater public demand for securities in India's capital market and thus encourage greater use of the capital market by private firms, as well as the government. On the supply side of that market the government took action to reduce controls over capital revenues by enterprises, to raise the maximum interest rate payable on certain types of debentures, to open the sale of equity shares to the public and to protect the interests of small investors in the securities market.[43]

F. A. Mehta, a senior executive of one of India's largest private enterprises—Tata Industries—and a leading industrial economist, provides a good summary of the opinion of enlightened large-scale private businessmen with respect to the reforms as of late 1986. After a brief summary of specific exemptions from control, significant tax reductions, and the reduction in the time required for clearances of licenses in certain industrial fields, he remarks,

> [Even] more conspicuously, the attitude of the Government in conducting open-house discussions with managers and indus-

trialists has created an overall milieu of confidence among them.

But . . . this is not to mean that controls have been dismantled . . . , they still remain a very powerful instrument. Nor has privatization . . . come into existence. [Privatization in India normally means that the government permits private-sector entry into specific areas formerly reserved to government.]

What, however is certainly true is that both Indian and foreign business enterprises in India no longer operate under the intensely emotional and hostile environment which prevailed during most of the decade of the 1970s. . . . The prevailing slogans in India are not ideological—they are managerial. They are those of 'efficiency' . . . 'modernization' and so on. . . . The Prime Minister's message of taking India into the twenty-first century . . . has had the effect of inviting a debate on . . . specific managerial solutions to the problems of the Indian economy. This managerial mood coincides with the temper of the emergent and enlarging middle class of India, which is no longer prepared to accept uncritically the [populist] slogans of the . . . decade [of the 1970s]."[44]

Mehta goes on to add that by late 1986, a reaction had set in to this liberalization. While he notes that some critics agree that it is not proceeding sufficiently quickly, there are other critics who feel that the liberalization policies are opposed to Indian socialism, and that they threaten Indian self-reliance. Furthermore, they are criticized for not helping to solve India's problems of unemployment and income distribution, and in fact they may exacerbate both. When inefficient firms fail, unemployment increases, while the beneficiaries of the reform seem to be members of a growing, but still minority, middle class. Mehta points out that the 1985 reform budget, which was considered "pro-rich," was succeeded by a 1986 antipoverty budget and cites this as support for a tendency toward equilibrium in India's democratic politics.[45]

An indication of that equilibrating tendency, to which Atul Kohli gives great importance, is the failure of Rajiv Gandhi in May 1985 to get a ratification of an economic policy statement from the Congress party that would have set the party firmly behind the reform steps he had taken. The Congress party did not accept the proposed statement, but modified it, and eventually ratified a resolution that "recommitted Rajiv and the Congress Party to socialism. . . . [This] underlined clearly and starkly that the government's economic policy will maintain continuity with the past, that socialism will define the limits within which new policies will have to fit."[46] Kohli goes on to point out the inconsistencies and confusion in the subsequent rhetoric and practice of reform as Gandhi and his associates sought to reassure the party and the public that the reforms were consistent with broad notions of Indian socialism. These include the maintenance of the public sector, tight limits on privatization, a stress upon poverty reduction, and a continued emphasis on national self-reliance in some sense.[47] This confusion contributed to the marginalization of further reform efforts from late 1985 onward and unquestionably played a major part in the government's unwillingness to present a white paper laying out a broad agenda of reform.

Despite this qualification, during the first two years of the liberalization, 1986–87, the prime minister and his secretariat put a great deal of pressure upon the bureaucracy to implement the reform policies. Enterprises in the areas in which reforms were stressed—exports, high-tech electronics and computers, cement, and certain consumer durables, among others—found that the permit impediments to entry and growth were relaxed. Capital issue and foreign exchange approvals were also expedited. Enterprises in lower-priority sectors however found little change in procedure.

But by mid-1987, Rajiv Gandhi's political problems had become more difficult. The electoral loss in Haryana in May 1987, the charges of corruption over the Bofors gun purchase, the departure of V. P. Singh from the cabinet, and the defection of other allies to the opposition undermined his popularity and political support. These occurrences also forced a greater reliance upon older Congress party leaders who had been shunted to one side in the euphoria of the 1985 election. Various other pressures arose to occupy the time and energy of the prime minister and economic reform lost its momentum. The power of the bureaucracy vis-à-vis the business sector was largely reestablished. There was worry among businessmen that the budgets of 1988 and 1989 might show backward steps on reform, and that they did not was seen as positive; in fact, as noted earlier, a further reduction of taxes on export profits was taken. The decision to permit Pepsi-Cola to invest jointly with a private Indian concern in a fruit processing plant in the strife-torn Punjab was taken against great pressure, though it was a positive step not only with respect to foreign investment but for Punjab's development. But this, too, was a more or less isolated action muted in its public announcement.

Several economists saw the failure of Gandhi to present his reform program in a well-integrated single package and document, but in a tentative manner, as placing the government in a defensive position. P. N. Dhar argued in 1986 that "a fuller and bolder reform program [including a forthright critique of old policies] . . . would have probably secured much greater political support for the reforms . . . [and] would have brought out the true nature of political resistance to the reforms."[48] A well-publicized, bold, integrated program would have enabled the government to better resist the piecemeal opposition of vested or ideological interests to particular reforms which could be individually opposed. In 1988 Dhar decried the absence of strong public debate on broad economic policy, and again urged the government to initiate such a debate in order to establish a well thought-out and coherent policy.[49]

A. Vaidyanathan, another of India's leading economists, struck a strong reinforcing note when he remarked on the inability "of the Indian State to articulate and impose an overall long term [economic] strategy" in the face of the "compulsion of competitive electoral politics" and the pressures of "various competing interest groups" upon "those involved in running the State." This weakness is shown in the area of industrial policy by the "lack of a coherent concept of . . . the relation between the State and private industry; [or] . . . a well thought out strategy to bring about the desired transformation. . . . At the moment, the process is caught up in the conflicts between industry and the regulating apparatus of the State [including both politicians and bureaucracy], and between different segments of industry. The crucial problem of insulating the public enterprises from bureaucratic and political interference, and giving greater autonomy to their management, is not even confronted, largely because this is against the interest of the political executive and the higher levels of bureaucracy."[50]

Thus we may conclude that on a dilemma posed by political scientists and economists, Kohli, a political scientist, stresses the ideological and self-interest resistances within the Congress party and the broader Indian polity that limited the areas and extent, and structured the process, of liberalizing reforms within India since 1980. He in effect argues that given the nature of the Indian political-economic system, marginal changes in economic policy were the only ones possible. The economists—Dhar, Guhan, and Vaidyanathan—argue that more fundamental change might have been possible within that system, and criticize India's then political leader Rajiv Gandhi for not taking advantage of his position and overwhelming victory in 1985 to present a well-articulated integrated reform program that would have initiated the debate necessary to carry through such a program. I will explore this disagreement and dilemma further when I look later at the Indian reform process within the Indian political system.

CONTRASTS

There are several major differences between the industrial reforms in China and India. The Chinese reform process began in the previously stagnant agricultural sector in terms of output, and the strongly positive results of the reform in that sector were a major factor in the demand for, and results of, the industrial reforms. The fundamental systemic change in agriculture that occurred in China was not possible in India because India had not undergone a previous unpopular collectivization, nor was an extensive land reform of ownership possible because of political constraints. Nor had India achieved the rural in-kind infrastructure investment that China had achieved by force via collectivization, and neither country had invested significantly in agricultural infrastructure from central budget funds. India's Green Revolution had occurred a decade previously, and rates of farm output and rural growth had subsequently returned to the steady, but low, long-term rate. Thus the demand for additional industrial output in India had to arise from either its urban population, or expanding foreign trade, rather than from its agricultural sector.

A second major difference was that the Chinese reforms sought to move from a highly centralized and planned system with no private sector, and a minimal institutional system for independent enterprise, to a less directed and planned system, with greater enterprise autonomy, while maintaining the leading role of the Communist party. The Indian system is far more flexible institutionally and did not require the fundamental changes that the Chinese system required. Rather it called for a program that would significantly improve the functioning of its ongoing system. India has not had a Cultural Revolution like China's, which decimated China's former political and economic leadership, destroyed existing institutions, and set back technical levels of education by a generation; as a result the pressures for change were nowhere near as great in India.

In both countries the goals of reforms were similar. The reforms themselves were directed at increasing the autonomy of the enterprise managers and increasing the profitability of the highly subsidized government-owned enterprise. In India, since many prices were already market determined, price reform was important but not central; in China it was a crucial element of the process. A major difference in the reforms was that the extended delegation of supervisory powers and finances to local and provincial agencies that occurred in China did not occur in India. Similarly the extent of decentralization of foreign trade was far greater in China than in India, arising in part from China's greater isolation from world technology and trade in the pre-reform era, resulting in greater pressures to open up following the reforms.

In both countries, too, the reforms were politically sensitive, evidenced by the initially tentative and experimental character of the two reform processes. The economic policy changes were recognized as reform programs only at a fairly late stage in each country, and even then with qualifications.

CHAPTER FOUR

Economic Results of the Reforms

The fundamental way to promote economic development lies in readjusting the industrial structure and the product mix. [Without that] we will continue to be immersed in the endless circulation of a 'chaos following relaxed control, tight control following the chaos, a deadlock following the tight control, and relaxed control following the deadlock' instead of achieving spiral development.

LI PENG, 1990

I N both China and India the economic reforms in the industrial field sought to improve incentives for more efficient and intensive use of resources by both enterprises and individuals as the major means of achieving the goals of the reforms: to raise industrial outputs, produce better quality products, and raise the technology levels in industry whether that industry was under government or private ownership. In the process the reforms were also intended to change the structure of industrial outputs to give greater weight to production of consumer goods relative to capital goods, and to exports relative to domestic production. Imports and foreign investment were also to be encouraged in order to improve quality and raise levels of technology. Did the reforms in fact do what they were intended to do at the sector and enterprise level, and then, did they have the desired macroeconomic results of accelerating growth or output, incomes, and employment?

CHINA

I concluded the discussions of China in the two previous chapters by quoting respectively from Ma Hong's analysis of China's industrial problems before the reforms, and from Zhao Ziyang's 1987 "Report to the Communist Party" on the pre-1987 reforms and reform proposals for the future. What were the effects of those reforms and Zhao Ziyang's proposals? How has the Chinese industrial system been functioning between the key 1984 urban reform resolution and the political crisis of the spring of 1989?[1]

First, the state reduced its mandatory role with respect to the industrial sector. The number of industrial products under state directive planning was cut from 131 in about 1979 to 14 in 1988, declining from 40 percent of the gross value of industrial output to about 20 percent; the number of products allocated by the state was reduced from 179 items in 1979 to 24 in 1988; petty commodities and products not encompassed by planning are now sold through the market. But among the key materials allocated according to plan in 1988 were steel (47 percent of the output of steel products), coal (44 percent of output), timber (26 percent), and cement (14 percent).[2]

Of the total sales turnover of products in 1988, about 50 percent was at prices set by the state and 50 percent at prices regulated by the market. The prices of agricultural products and industrial consumer goods set by the state dropped respectively to 30 percent and 40 percent of their total turnover. Many of the products were priced by the state exchange under a two-track price system, with the planned part of the output sold at state-set prices and output above the plan sold at floating market prices, which may be substantially higher.[2]

For enterprise management in the state sector a contract responsibility system was introduced. Normally three-to-five-year contracts are given to managers along the lines indicated in the previous chapter. This contract system is one that "does not break with the traditional ownership system, or disturb vested interests, [so that] . . . it is rather easy to implement. . . . [It] encourages people to cherish public property as . . . their own."

China has also adopted a variety of other ownership patterns "on condition that state ownership remains dominant." In the late 1970s enterprises under public ownership produced 80 percent of the total value of industrial output; this had fallen to 57.5 percent by the mid-1980s. Over the same period of time the output of the collective sector (i.e., cooperatively owned), had grown from 20 percent of industrial output to 40 percent; and a reestablished private sector was producing 2.3 percent of the total in contrast to a negligible amount in the 1970s. In the commercial sector commerce via agencies under public ownership had fallen from 90 percent of the total turnover to 39 percent; the share of the collective sector had risen from 7 percent to 36 percent, while that of the private and joint sectors had risen from 3 percent to 26 percent. By 1988–89, there were seventeen million employees in the private industrial and commercial sectors—which was over 100 times the level of such employment in the 1970s.

Apart from decision making over direct production and distribution of output, enterprise and local decision-making power over fixed-asset investments also expanded greatly. In 1978 the central state budget financed 77 percent of capital construction investment. By 1987 only 32 percent of such investment was so financed, with the remaining 68 percent coming from other sources such as enterprise funds, local government budgets, and banks.

The positive effect of reforms giving enterprises greater autonomy has been to press managers to lay greater stress upon profitability as a goal. This has forced them to adapt their enterprise production plans to changing market demands and make greater efforts to market their products, as well as to use their inputs more economically than previously. The consumption of energy and of steel products in production fell significantly during much of the reform decade, and industrial output grew at a somewhat more rapid rate than previously. There was also a massive increase in industrial exports, the volume of foreign trade, and the number and value of foreign investment and loan contracts. There was an especially rapid growth of industrial output by village and township enterprises in rural areas, which accompanied the initial rural reforms and later urban ones. Such output grew at a rate of almost 30 percent per year from 1979 to 1986, and that sector's share of China's larger total industrial output more than tripled over the same time period.[4]

But the process of reform contained within itself the seeds of a series of subsequent problems, which China has not yet resolved, and which probably contributed to the political crises of mid-1989. Luo Yianzheng, in his prophetic article, points out the "coexistence of a dual [economic] structure and dual economic mechanisms [that] has occurred with in-depth reform. . . . On the one hand, certain old system regulations and controls—the highly centralized management of the product economy with administrative measures as the main tools—have become weak or even disappeared. On the other hand, the new system—management of the planned commodity economy—has not yet been completely set up and perfected, hence some failures in overall control and . . . lack of internal coordination. Reform now faces a dilemma: economic activities can neither still be controlled by administrative directives nor guided or regulated effectively by economic means. It is difficult to avoid instability and lack of coordination in the economy without resolving the antagonism between the new and old systems."[5]

As examples of such conflicts he notes that enterprises can increase profits by opting "for planned prices through the planning channel . . . [and simultaneously seizing] the 'profit' of negotiated prices by access to markets." Furthermore the relatively short terms of the contracts contribute to a short-term vision on the part of the management, when a longer-term approach might be preferable. Too, while the contract system has given managers greater autonomy, "enterprises have not yet obtained real corporation status and it is difficult to rationalize their behavior. . . . [An] enterprise is responsible only for its profits but not for its losses. . . . [If it] suffers losses or goes bankrupt it is still the State which carries the responsibility. . . . [Thus] weak financial restraint [at the enterprise level] leads to weak budget restraint."[6] In fact, in 1987 during the first three months, 8,900 state-owned industrial enterprises—23 percent of the number in the national budget—were operating with a total loss exceeding $400 million; and the number of such loss-making enterprises was 900 more than in the same period of 1986. The 1987 draft state budget allocated over a quarter of state expenditures for subsidies to cover enterprise losses and to compensate consumers for price increases. The budgeted subsidies for state enterprises as of mid-1988 were expected to equal almost half of the national industrial profits from all such enterprises.[7]

Another aspect of the reforms to increase enterprise autonomy that has stimulated industrial activity but also contributed to serious economic problems is the devolution of financial authority and resources from the central government to the enterprise itself, and to the government of the locality in which it operates. One of the obvious purposes of allowing enterprises to retain a significant portion of their profits was to give them greater control of their own investment decisions, as well as to provide rewards to staff and workers from that profitable performance. But apparently there has been little relationship between changes in the productivity of labor in an enterprise and the profitability of that enterprise.

Profitability is in fact far more influenced by the firm's fixed asset position than by its workers' productivity. But without a labor market and job mobility, workers cannot move to new jobs in response to offers of higher wages from more profitable enterprises. Therefore workers in profitable state enterprises put their managers under great pressure to give bonuses and wage hikes from profits, and to spread these among all workers in the firm on a more or less equal basis. In addition, "[when] wages in one sector shoot up, workers in every other enterprise . . . press for 'matching' wage hikes."[8] Such demands for matching wage hikes to workers in enterprises that may

not be as profitable as those in the initiating sector are looked at sym-
pathetically by factory managers, local governments, and other
higher-up agencies because these supervisors wish to maintain a satisfied labor force, since an unhappy labor force can make it difficult
for managers. Enterprises are thus under pressure to use retained
profits for higher wages and bonuses. To grant these they have been
able "through negotiations with . . . higher ups to [both] raise the percentage of retained profits in gross profit . . . , and to [significantly]
increase the percentage of bonus disbursement in retained profit."[9]

There are also numerous loopholes in the enterprise accounting
system that enable enterprises to dodge wage controls and to provide
greater bonuses and benefits. Such "upward emulation" and higher
wages in turn trigger substantial increases in welfare fund expenditures within an enterprise. On a national level the effect has been to
increase funds for consumption demand "far ahead of the level of production." Luo Yuanzheng regards this competitive emulation to be a
remainder of the pre-reform wage system of "egalitarianism and eating from the same big pot. . . . The consequences of this [in the new
situation] is a series of 'imitative effects' [with respect to both investment and consumption], and many [enterprises] go along with the
tide to raise prices."[10]

As profit retention by the enterprise has contributed to rising
pressure for higher wages and benefits and ultimately higher product
costs and prices, the devolution of decision making and profit retention from the center to the local authority also has had significant
micro- and macro- consequences. This devolution reinforced and
legitimized tendencies that already existed before the reforms.
Dorothy Solinger concludes that many of the market-oriented reforms with respect to such matters, among others, as property rights,
bankruptcy, and bidding on construction, have led to the creation of
new local bureaucratic organs between the individual enterprise and
the new market institutions. The purpose of these new agencies is to
make certain that the results of the market activities are consistent
with local government interests. "[Administrative] interference and
direct controls still persist and local authorities . . . try to widen
areas of directive planning." Conflicts and friction have been encouraged by the new "management at every level" system, and protective
economic blockades have been introduced in some areas.[11]

Hussain adds that this closer relationship between local governments and local enterprises is not simply a carryover of the old system, but "also rests on mutual dependence. . . . [Enterprises] are the
most important source of revenue . . . for local government . . . [and
these] local and provincial governments only derive revenue from [lo-

cal] enterprises. . . . [The tax system too] is more like revenue sharing through case by case bargaining than a system of taxation."[12] On the other side, enterprises perform many social welfare functions which are elsewhere the responsibility of the governments. Thus local governments depend highly for funds and services on local enterprises, but the enterprises also depend on those governments. "[The] government is still the largest commercial intermediary. Many of the important inputs can only be acquired through the government. Similarly . . . enterprises need the help of government to obtain bank credit. . . . [Enterprise] reforms until now have concentrated on the formal transfer of decision-making to enterprises; they have not set out to alter the economic and social factors which sustain the mutual dependence of the government and enterprises."[13]

A major effect of this devolution of revenues and spending authority from the center to lower levels has been the great increase in noncentral budget funds. (These are the revenues that have been shifted to the regional governments, plus the net income after taxes of enterprises.) Such nonbudget funds rose by almost five times in absolute amounts between 1978 and 1987, growing from 14 percent of the 1979 national income to 21 percent of the greater 1986 income. Over the same period the central government's budget revenues only doubled absolutely, while its expenditures for such current expenses as subsidies for farmers and urban workers and to make up for enterprise losses have increased markedly. The result has been a reduction in budgeted funds for investment. Another consequence of these revenue and expenditure trends has been that the central budgets from 1986 to 1989 had regular annual deficits which were in effect met by creating money. The supply of money increased by about 12 percent per year from 1981 to 1987, but in 1988 this accelerated sharply, with an increase in money supply on the order of 47 percent, and there was a similar tendency in early 1989. Another result of this devolution of funding has been that the share of fixed investment financed by the central budget fell from 75–80 percent of the total in 1975–78 to less than one-third by 1987. The nonbudget fixed investment is of course far less under the control of the central government than the budgeted investment. Much of the former has been used either for final consumption-oriented purposes, such as housing, or for investment in industries to produce consumer-durable goods such as television sets, washing machines, and refrigerators to meet provincial goals.[14]

Another related result of the investment boom, which in large part reflects the small retained reserve funds of local enterprises and the desires of local governments to establish local industries, together with the absence of financial markets to pool funds, has been the "miniaturization" of unit investment scale. "The reality we are facing today . . . is the expansion of gross investment coupled with a decline in scale." As examples of this tendency the authors of the China Economic System Reform Research Institute (CESRRI) survey cite the existence of 130 washing-machine factories in the country in 1984, of which only 9 were of the minimum optimal annual production scale of 200,000 units; of 110 refrigerator factories, with an average output of 4,600 units per year, far below "the rational scale"; and of over 110 motorcar factories, with an average scale of production of 2,000 cars per year. " 'Short term and quick turnover' has become a principle governing the choice of investment targets." The authors believe this investment has been at the expense of necessary longer-term and larger investment, in such infrastructure areas as energy, and transport and in the modernization of China's relatively old metallurgical industry, 85 percent of whose equipment goes back to the 1960s and earlier.[15]

On the positive side, the especially rapid growth of industrial output from the collectively owned village and township enterprises (VTE) in the rural sector reflects the success of the introduction of the household responsibility system in agriculture in raising rural incomes and demand, and of the devolution of financial resources and investment decisions to the local government. Both "peasants and local government [are responding positively] to the institutional and economic framework within which they operate [since the agricultural reform]."[16] In one insightful study of what has happened to wool production and processing in rural Yulin prefecture, the authors point out that the peasants responded in their production decisions very closely to the changes in the market for wool. This operated under tight price controls until 1985, when the lifting of the controls led to subsequent sharp price rises. Over the same period "[the] dismantling of the communes made it essential for rural party cadres to find alternative sources of income. In many areas cadres were the driving force in the establishment of local manufacturing establishments."[17] Establishing a plant to process the greater supply of wool was one possibility. The devolution of financial resources and power over funds to local officials and organizations provided the funds to set up such a plant—and the result was the construction of a fine wool factory in Yulin prefecture. It was hoped that this would "generate sources of local revenue and local employment. [But] . . . it was constructed . . . with very imperfect knowledge of parallel developments taking place elsewhere in the country. The inevitable results of . . . these diverse development efforts [throughout China] have been an extraordinary growth in productive capacity [in wool processing], a . . . scramble for a share of a static quantity of raw material [in the short run], and a prices explosion."[18]

The VTEs manufacture not only wool, as in the above case, but a variety of other consumer goods, as well as machines, chemicals, and metals. In the manufacture of some of these they compete with state-owned industries for inputs and skilled personnel. They are far more flexible than the large state enterprises, since the workers are village inhabitants who do not receive the social welfare benefits supplied to workers in the state-owned factories, but who rather live in their own homes, and use the village health and education facilities. Since the workers, as village inhabitants, may share in the collective owner-ship of the enterprise, they have a strong incentive for the enterprise to be profitable. Jacobs notes that in each of the localities he visited, "employment in industry is two to three times more renumerative than in agriculture. Thus the men in a family may take industrial jobs leaving the women to perform agricultural work." He remarks too on "the continuing political control of economic affairs," despite new institutions formally separating the party and the government from economic organs.[19]

Because of the flexibility and lower overhead social costs of VTEs, as well as their ability to find land on which to expand at a low cost, a large urban factory may often find that it can expand output more readily by subcontracting parts of its operations to such a rural plant than by trying to expand its own plant. Simpler components of a final product, which can be produced by relatively unskilled workers using less complex equipment and supervised by retired skilled personnel from the larger plant, are subcontracted by large state plants in Shang-hai and Nanjing to VTEs. There is no size limit for such collective enterprises and many employ hundreds of workers.

The total rural township enterprise sector (township village and private—TVP) has been described as "the most dynamic part of Chinese industry" at least until 1986. "Its share in total national GVIO [Gross Value of Industrial Output] has risen from . . . 9 percent on the eve of the reforms in 1978 . . . to more than 21 percent in 1986. . . . [Within this TVP sector the share of] private enter-prises . . . rose from negligible levels in the late 1970s to account for nearly 5 percent of China's GVIO in 1986." In addition, the rural labor employed in industry grew from 19 million workers in 1980 to 31 mil-lion in 1986, or from 6 to 8 percent of the growing total rural labor force.[20]

There is apparently an interesting division of labor between the collectively owned rural enterprises and the privately owned ones. The former flourished in the rural areas near the large urban industrial centers, such as southern Jiangsu province near Shanghai and Nanjing, doing a good deal of subcontracting for the large state-owned urban enterprises. The private enterprises grew more rapidly in the less-developed regions of the country, manufacturing products for local needs often from locally grown raw materials. Perhaps reflecting this difference, as well as ideological issues relating to employment by private firms, the privately owned individual enterprises averaged 2 workers (including the employer) per enterprise, in contrast to 18 workers in a collectively owned brigade enterprise and 50 workers in a collectively owned commune enterprise.[21]

Questions have arisen with respect to the economic efficiency of these smaller enterprises, although their rate of return on capital may be higher than for larger firms. Many were established to meet local demands, and may depend for their revenues on their isolation or on protected markets, despite diseconomies of scale and the existence of numerous potential competitors.[22] This suspicion may have contributed to the central government's clampdown on such enterprises in 1988 and 1989, as part of its program to both control unbudgeted investment in an inflationary period, and reduce the competition for inputs between this TVP sector and the state-owned industries.

Keeping in mind the limited investment funds left to enterprises from their revenues as a result of competing wage and welfare demands, and considering the fiscal constraints on local governments, where did the funds come from to finance the VTEs and this large volume of extrabudgetary investment? Banks have become another major source of investment funds. With "investment decision-makers [who] are . . . not afraid of bankruptcy," there was no reluctance on the part of enterprises to go to banks for credit;[23] local governments were able to borrow easily. Bank lending increased by about 30 billion yuan per year from 1979 to 1984; but in 1985 this increase grew to 100 billion yuan and in the three years from 1986 to 1988 the annual increase in bank loans averaged 150 billion yuan. As of the end of 1987 the banking system had 900 billion yuan in loans outstanding, of which almost 500 billion yuan were for circulating capital.[24] "But . . . there is a large amount of loans over due. . . . [A] considerable amount of loaned circulation capital [was] used for the fixed capital investments. This is because the banks are not independent from government and cannot refuse the requests for loans by it. . . . In addition, the banks lack strict regulations [with] regard to . . . the time for repayment and conditions for renewing. Furthermore, banks at present, are not profit making institutions [with signed contracts with the government] in regard to profit and loss in their operations

. . . as most [industrial] enterprises on the contract responsibility system. All these led to . . . [an] easy condition for credit expansion."[25] The increase in credit and money supply resulted in a general increase in the official retail price and cost-of-living indices on the order of 35–40 percent from 1985 to 1988, of which over half occurred in the last year, 1987–88. (The rise in the free market price indices for consumer goods was about half again as rapid.)[26]

An increase in economic irregularities and corruption has also accompanied the reforms. "The economic reforms have cut the ground from many of the erstwhile canons of virtuous conduct. . . . 'To be rich is glorious.' . . . Asceticism in personal consumption is . . . an aberration from a superseded era. . . . Many of the major economic reforms have been introduced by creating a 'state of exception' . . . irregular, if not outright illegal. . . . They have been initiated . . . by . . . exempting selected regions, enterprises or activities from the usual regulations and laws. . . . [This] does create legal and procedural vacuums and blind spots in policing. . . . [Finally] reliance on personal relationships or status to gain preferential access to goods and jobs is regarded as unfair . . . by many Chinese, yet . . . most resort to it . . . to gain access to ordinary goods and services."[27]

One of the reforms of the price system—the introduction of the two-track system—made it possible to make substantial gains by resale of scarce, price-controlled goods. "Prior to the reforms goods [obtained through personal contacts or status] could only be for own-use. Individuals could not sell their spoils. . . . The opening of private markets has made resales possible, thus increasing the economic value of goods obtained through contacts or status [both to individuals and to enterprises, which now have financial autonomy]. . . . [Since 1985 the] growth of personal incomes has created a captive market for consumption goods not readily available in the shops [and] . . . there is an excess demand for production goods and building materials fanned by the rapid rate of growth of the economy. . . . There is thus a propitious environment for a large number of people to make a living out of buying and selling goods for a quick profit." Too, while the reforms have reduced the range and detail of administrative controls, there is still "a wide latitude left to administrative discretion together with [an] informality of administrative routines . . . [that] has made it possible for Party cadres and officials to misuse their powers for personal gain."[28]

Thus an economic system that differs from the system that functioned in China before 1978 was created by the reforms. The new system combines greater autonomy for enterprises, with a greater devolution of authority to the local level than in the past; it also contains an active banking system that has become the major source of investment funding. But it still retains large elements of administrative discretion on the part of government and party officials at the local level as well as the national level, in part because of the absence of an effective tax system; it lacks a working macroeconomic system to control the supply of credit and more broadly money; and it does not have in place a public system to provide the social benefits such as housing, education, and welfare currently provided by the industrial system, or the protection against unemployment that lifetime employment provided to industrial workers.

The reformed system achieved many of the macroeconomic goals of the reformers. There has been a doubling of the growth rate of China's net material product from about 4 percent per year in the previous two decades to almost 9 percent from 1976 to 1985.[29] Peasant incomes more than tripled between 1978 and 1987, while urban incomes more than doubled. Obviously such orders of increase reflect the exceptionally sharp increase in the annual agricultural growth rate, which rose from about 4 percent in the 1970–77 period to over 10 percent from 1978 to 1986, and which was in large part a product of the agricultural reforms. Within that overall agricultural growth rate the output of conventional agricultural products (grains, cash crops, timber, animals, and fish) rose by 7 percent per year, while industrial output produced by the VTEs grew by 30 percent per year. By 1986 such VTE output had risen to 40 percent of the value of the nonindustrial output produced by the agricultural sector, compared to only 15 percent before the reforms.[30]

The increase in urban incomes reflects in part the continued, but somewhat accelerated, high rates of industrial growth. The overall annual growth rate for industry rose from 11 percent in 1970–77 to 13 percent for 1978–88.[31] Within those overall averages the growth rate of heavy industry, producing capital goods, remained roughly constant at 12 percent in both periods. The goal had been to reduce that rate. But the annual growth rate of light industry, producing consumer goods and hand tools, rose from 10 percent to 15 percent between the same two time periods, and has been consistently higher than the growth rate for heavy industry after 1978. The net effect was a quadrupling of the output of light industrial products compared to a less than three-fold increase in heavy industry output from 1978 to 1988. This has certainly been consistent with the reformers' goal of greater consumer goods output, relative to that of investment goods. Some of this increase in consumer durable goods output is shown in table 1.

With such increases in outputs of consumer goods the avail-

TABLE 1.
Output of selected consumer durable goods, 1978 and 1985

Product	Output (in 000 units)	
	1978	1985
Sewing machines	500	1,000
Bicycles	8,500	30,000
Watches	13,500	54,000
Household refrigerators	28	1,400
Household washing machines	1	8,900
Electric fans	1,400	31,700
Radio sets	12,000	16,000[a]
Television sets	520	17,000
Recorders	50	1,400
Cameras	180	1,800

Source: PRC, Statistical Yearbook of China, 1986, pp. 246–48. Table of "Output of Major Industrial Products." I have rounded the figures in that table.

[a] Radio set production reached a peak of 41 million units in 1981.

ability of consumer durable goods per peasant household in China also rose sharply between 1978 to 1985. The number of more conventional consumer durables—bicycles, sewing machines, radios, and clocks—per 100 peasant households rose by two or three times in that period, the number of wristwatches by over four times; television sets per 100 households rose from less than one to twelve in that short time.[32] In addition to these light products, output of such heavy industrial products as plate glass and cement, both used in housing, doubled from 1978 to 1985, while that of motor vehicles (largely trucks) and small tractors almost tripled over the same period, undoubtedly as a result of greater rural household demand (output of large tractors fell).

The relative decline in the weight of heavy industry subsector was consistent with the reform policies to reduce the share of accumulation (investment) in national income in order to make more available for consumption, while raising the productivity of capital in order to maintain high growth rates. It was also recognized that a shift in investment to the consumer goods sector and to agriculture would be necessary to expand outputs from those sectors; to break the bottlenecks in such infrastructure sectors as power and transport, as well as education, also called for investment. The past population growth and failure to construct housing had resulted in a shortage of housing. There was a large pent-up demand for more and better housing in both the cities and rural areas, which was also fueled by the higher post-1980 incomes. (Investment in services and housing is classified as "nonproductive" in Marxist terminology.)

Some of these desired shifts did occur but others did not. Accumulation as a share of national income did fall from about 35–37 per cent in 1978 to a range of 28–30 percent in the 1981–83 period. But from 1984 on it climbed, again reaching about 35 percent during 1985–88. As noted earlier, this rise reflected the delegation of investment-making powers to enterprises and local governments, which they were able to use by going to the banks for loans. Also significant is the increasing share of consumption investment in housing in the total capital construction. Housing rose from less than 12 percent of capital construction in 1976–80 to over 20 percent in 1981–85, before falling to 14 percent of the larger total in 1986–88. In the urban areas this increase reflected larger investment by enterprises for welfare; in rural areas greater household investment.[33]

Apart from consumption investment for housing, the share of investment in light industry remained roughly stable at about 6 percent of the total from 1978 to 1988, except for a rise in 1980–82. Heavy industry's share of total investment fell from 46 percent in 1976–80 to about 35–40 percent in 1981–88, counterbalancing the rise in housing. But within the total industrial investment the share for technical innovation and transformation rose from 1978 to 1985, while that for new facilities fell somewhat. Contrary to the hope for greater agricultural investment, the share of agriculture in the total declined steadily from about 10 percent in 1978–79 to 3 percent in 1985 and 1988. In fact the absolute level of investment in agriculture fell in the 1980s compared to the 1970s. There was some increase in the shares of energy and transport in total capital construction, with their combined shares rising from one-third in the 1976–80 period to 35–40 percent in the later 1980s; the absolute investment in both sectors rose significantly.

Thus to summarize the effects of the reform on investment, there was no decline in investment as a share of total output; there was no increase in the shares of investment for consumer goods production whether in agriculture or light industry; there was some decline in heavy industry's share, which was counterbalanced by the substantial increase in investment for housing and infrastructure; and there was some shift in investment for modernization as opposed to new construction. The one sector in which there was an absolute decline in investment was in agriculture; in all others absolute investment rose, reflecting higher output and investment totals.

An important component of the reform package to raise efficiency and productivity of industry was the continued opening up of the economy to foreign technology and products through greater foreign trade and investment. Foreign trade grew rapidly.[34] Exports rose from a level of about $7 billion per year in the 1974–76 period to $31 billion in 1986, and then leaped to $48 billion in 1988. Imports were slightly above exports in 1974–76, but by 1986 they had risen to $43 billion and then to $55 billion in 1988. In the 1970s China's exports were less than 6 percent of its total output; by 1986 they were 14 percent of the higher output. Furthermore, China moved from a rough balance in its current trade account in the 1970s to a deficit high of $15 billion in 1985 that fell to $8 billion in 1988.

In this rapidly growing foreign-trade sector Hong Kong played a major role as a direct market for China's exports, as a supplier of imports, and as an intermediary to third countries, including South Korea and Taiwan, with whom direct trade by China was greatly restricted for political reasons. Hong Kong took about 20–25 percent of the value of China's exports from 1978 to 1985, while its role as a supplier of imports rose from less than 1 percent in 1977–78 to about 20 percent in 1985. Close to 60 percent of China's exports to Hong Kong were reexported, reflecting outputs of enterprises set up by Hong Kong investors in China for eventual export to third countries, including Taiwan and South Korea. A substantial portion of the value of Hong Kong's exports to China was for machinery and inputs for those same enterprises, including inputs from Taiwan and South Korea. Hong Kong's entrepreneurs, as investors and traders, thus played a key role in China's opening to the outer world.[35]

During the early part of the reform period a significant portion of the greater imports were of consumer durable products. With higher rural and urban incomes the increased demand for such products could not be met from domestic production rapidly, while at the same time it was politically important to make durable consumer goods available to the people to tangibly encourage and reward greater effort and productivity. Thus legal imports of consumer durables rose from about 1 percent of total imports in 1978 to more than 5 percent in 1984 and 1985 before falling as a share in 1986, though probably rising absolutely. There is evidence too of increasing semilegal or illegal imports by local governments or enterprises which saw a chance of making profits from such transactions. But the main reason for the decline in consumer durables as a share of total imports was unquestionably the increasing domestic production of those items as investment in their domestic production rose, combined with restrictions on their import in recent years.

In addition to the greater consumer durable imports, which remain minor in the share of total imports, a major shift in the import pattern has been the growing importance of capital goods. These grew from less than 20 percent of total imports in the 1970s to over 40 percent in 1985–86. At the same time imports of industrial inputs (chemicals, raw materials, and metals) declined from two-thirds of the total to about 40–45 percent (still slightly more than capital goods) in 1985–86. Harding regards this as a significant sign of China's move away from self-sufficiency and its lessening fear of dependency.[36]

On the export side what is very significant is the steady increase in the share of manufacturing exports in the total, the steady decline in agricultural exports, and the rise in extractive exports—crude oil and petroleum products—from 1978 to 1985; but the share of the latter group declined sharply from 1985 to 1986. Two significant elements in this greater role of manufactured exports than in the past are the export of higher value textile products, especially clothing, as opposed to fibers and yarns, and the export of weapons, which by 1982–86 had risen to about 5 percent of China's total exports and over 10 percent of its manufactured exports. A revealing indication of China's success in expanding its manufactured exports is that by 1990 it had achieved a surplus of $10.4 billion in its trade with the United States.[37]

Not surprisingly, as part of its opening to the world, China has greatly increased its receptivity to tourists. The number of non-Chinese foreign tourists increased from about 500,000 in 1980 to over 1.8 million in 1988, while the numbers of overseas Chinese tourists (including those from Hong Kong, Macao, and Taiwan) has risen from below 2 million to almost 30 million. Earnings from tourism rose from $260 million in 1978 to $2.3 billion in 1988. Somewhat more surprising for a Marxist country, China has also begun exporting labor services, especially to other developing countries, and earnings from such export services reached almost a billion dollars in 1986.[38]

In 1979 China adopted a foreign investment law that established a legal basis for direct investment by foreign firms. At first restrictions were placed on the type, area, and sectors of such investment, but gradually these were widened, so that now such investment is welcome throughout the country with few restrictions. The total of direct foreign investment actually made from 1979 to 1985 was $6.0 billion, which was approximately 40 percent of the $16.0 billion of investment contracted. The value of contracts for investment increased in every year after 1979, at least until 1988. There is however reason to believe that the investments have not been in the high-technology area hoped for, and that the basic issues of access by foreign investors to the domestic market and their ability to repatriate local currency profits earned in that market in foreign exchange have not been resolved. There are also significant difficulties in transacting business and carrying out production in China that have discouraged investment. As a result actual direct investment may have fallen on an annual basis even before the Tiananmen Square incident in June 1989.[39] Despite these changes, Harding concludes that both foreign trade and investment remain highly regulated with policies in both areas directed toward a goal of "producing as much at home as possible . . . [with] foreign economic relationships that will, in the end, help produce a relatively self-reliant nation."[40]

Has industrial efficiency improved in the decade of the 1980s compared to earlier periods? One of the main purposes of the economic reforms was to go from the earlier process of extensive growth, in which total industrial growth was simply a product of growing inputs of factors of production, to one of intensive growth, in which growth would occur because of improvements in technology and the more efficient use of factor inputs. Efforts have been made to measure changes in factor productivities of Chinese industry, but this is extremely difficult; results disagree and what follows should be accepted with a great deal of caution. There is also no evidence of a direct relationship between specific reforms and productivity changes.

Various 1980–86 studies of productivity *in state owned industry,* using unrevised Chinese data, concluded that there had been little if any increase in multifactor productivity in that sector over the entire 1953–1985 period. While there had been a rapid rise in productivity during the 1953–57 First Five-Year Plan period, this was followed by an underlying stagnancy with periodic improvements and declines until the early 1980s. But in 1988, on the basis of revised data, which adjusts for industrial investment for housing and welfare activities as well as for the labor forces in those activities, and thus better measures the capital and labor actually used in industrial production, Chen Kuan and his colleagues, together with G. H. Jefferson and T. G. Rawski, estimated a long-term annual growth rate of productivity, using a Cobb-Douglas production function, of 0.4 percent from 1957–78, with varying peaks and declines. This productivity growth rate rose to 1.9 percent from 1978 to 1983. The authors conclude that "[The] post-1978 shift in the relative contribution of factor accumulation and productivity growth represents a dramatic departure from the previous 25 years of . . . factor-extensive growth . . . to [a period of] productivity driven growth. . . . [This is] in sharp contrast to [previous] studies . . . reporting no response to reform policies intended to shift Chinese industry onto a new path of intensive or productivity-led growth." If this study is reasonably correct it also indicates that while in the period until 1978 the growth of China's factor productivity in industry was well below the average for many other developing countries, in the period since 1978 it has been closer to that international average.[41]

While the reforms have achieved significant improvements in output and well-being since 1978, they have not eliminated the sharp fluctuations in the Chinese economy. However, since 1978 these have not resulted from sharp ideological swings and resulting policy changes by the leadership and the party. Rather they have been more a product of the gaps in the reformed system that resulted from the devolution of authority and control of funds to enterprises, local governments, and banks without establishing an effective central macroeconomic control system, using financial and taxation tools, that could effectively govern the broad contours of the economic behavior of those semi-independent economic agencies. Instead the central government relies in practice on discretionary administrative controls during periods of stability, and crash centralized controls in times of crises. The fluctuations in prices, culminating in their accelerated rise from 1987 to 1989, together with the greater sense of corruption and irregularities in the system that is popularly associated with the reforms, have created serious problems within Chinese society. It was estimated that in 1987 the real income of an estimated 21 percent of urban wage earners dropped as a result of the price rise.[42] The continued price rises and panic buying that followed the 1988 price reform led to a quick retraction of that reform, and rebounded to the political disadvantage of Zhao Ziyang and the more active reformers in the party. Luo Yuanzheng, writing shortly before the June 1989 Tiananmen Square incident, cautioned that price reform must "take into account the carrying capacity of society and the absorptive capacity of enterprises, otherwise reform will lose its social support."[43] He went on to discuss some of the broader social issues related to the Chinese reform process:

> Reform, as a social transformation, will necessarily result in friction and reallocation of interests among various social strata and groups. Heated arguments over "fairness and efficiency" are a prominent manifestation of this problem . . .
> For a long time, egalitarianism prevailed as the principle of equity under socialism . . . it was the spiritual force of moral

concepts, rather than material interests, that drove the economy. As a result, popular enthusiasm and creativity were
seriously fettered, . . . and the whole economy moved inefficiently. . . . Since [December 1978] . . . China had adopted a
policy to allow some people to get rich first. Uniform allocation
has been replaced gradually by differential allocation according
to work and the coexistence of various forms of allocation. This
policy has produced markedly stimulating results [especially]
in . . . the rural economy and private industrial and commercial
sectors. . . . The efficiency of . . . operations is being enhanced
while income levels of . . . citizens are also being raised. Meanwhile, the gap between the rich and the poor is also being
widened. [Some households earn ten thousand yuan, and even
millions while] . . . on the other hand, the lowest 15 percent are
unable to make ends meet. Moreover the gap between rich [de-
veloped coastal areas] and poor [borderland] areas is also being
widened. These phenomena have aroused widespread concern
and controversy. [There is an awareness too that opportunities
are not being made available equally to all people under the new
system.] . . . [People] are now not only dissatisfied with price
rises, but also with seeking profits through power, with appointments by favoritism, with lack of freedom to choose professions,
unequal incomes and so on, which are all related to unequal opportunities. . . . Because of the coexistence of new and old
systems [there are many distortions in structures and prices]
which result in unreasonable income inequalities. [This calls for
government intervention in the form of economic, legal and administrative macro-controls to prevent such polarization.]⁴⁴

The overall economic reform process had in fact been put on hold
since late 1988, after the collapse of the price reform. The central government moved to reduce the inflationary price rise by reimposing
further direct controls on the economy with respect to prices, investment, and the autonomy of regions and enterprises, especially in the
collective and private sector, and by reducing money supply and consumption funding. This did have the effect of reducing the inflation
rate somewhat in 1989; the rate of increase of industrial output also
declined to 7 percent in 1989, less than half that in 1988, and overall
growth to 4 percent. Many rural private enterprises were closed; some
rural collective enterprises were also closed, and more were apparently merged, with unemployment in them rising by about 600,000
(far less than feared). But in early 1990 there seems to be some evidence of both monetary relaxation in the form of higher wages, which
apparently stimulated a moderately higher growth rate, and a loosening of controls in some of the provinces and localities. In an August
1990 review of the current economic problems in China, Premier Li

Peng pointed out that there had been some increase in the rate of industrial growth in the first half of 1990 compared to 1989. There was also a sharp decline in the annual rate of retail price increase from about 18 percent in both 1988 and 1989 to only 3 percent in 1990. But despite this control of inflation, people's consumption of manufactured goods had declined. Li Peng reemphasized the need for China to move from a policy of growth for growth's sake to one of structural readjustment that stressed new technology, greater efficiency, and producing for the market. Otherwise China would not break out of what has been a vicious cycle of relaxed controls, chaos, tight controls, deadlock, and again relaxed controls.[45]

But in spite of short-term tightening and relaxation and perhaps an easing of the situation, Dong Fureng, writing in late 1988, pointed out the longer-term political issues arising from the "tough struggle" and "complexity of [economic] reform." He stressed that "major reform measures should be discussed extensively and understood thoroughly by the people . . . to avoid errors in policy making. The people should be told of difficulties and errors in reform as they really are. . . . [They] should understand that although reform will benefit them, the reform requires them to pay a certain price, or even make a temporary sacrifice; while party and government leaders should share weal and woe with the people. Democracy and openness in political affairs can enhance social unity. . . . China cannot closely coordinate the late start and slow progress in its political structural reform with its economic structure reform. . . . Special efforts should be made to accelerate the pace . . . on political structural reform."[46] This obviously did not occur in mid-1989.

INDIA

As in the discussion of the effects of industrial reforms in China, I will first examine the effects of the reforms in India on firms and industrial sectors, and then conclude by looking at the macroeconomic results.[47] In India, as in China, there was no early overall white paper by the government that presented the rationale for the reform program, or in fact such a program. The Indian Seventh Five-Year Plan did some of this in a limited sense, but there was no Congress party equivalent to China's 1984 Communist party statement. Rather the reforms were ad hoc changes in various parts of the existing system of regulations and controls, with the framework of the system remaining more or less intact. As in China the goals of these reforms were to achieve greater industrial growth than in the past and keep abreast of the advances in industrial technology elsewhere in the world, in order to raise living standards within India and maintain India's world political position.

Again as in China one of the major areas of reform was to expand the autonomy of enterprises, but unlike China, India has a large private industrial sector. Thus in India one of the directions of reform has been to ease the controls on private firms in both their current output mix of related products and their entry into new fields of production. In the public sector the reforms sought to give the managers greater freedom from ministerial and political controls in the operations of their firms, by such measures as Memoranda of Understanding (MOU) setting forth performance targets. A major intention was that these public enterprises make greater profits and become significantly larger contributors of resources to the government in the future than in the past.

The effect of the licensing reforms removed the need for central licensing for two-thirds of projects formerly subject to licensing; projects of a size below Rs. 500 million (approximately $30 million) located in industrially backward areas were in effect open to all would-be investors. (State and local government requirements on local zoning, etc. were of course not waived.) As a result many new business enterprises were set up in "sunrise" industries in which scale economies are not critical—television production and detergent production have been two such industries. T. N. Ninan remarks that "there is little doubt that the base of business entrepreneurship has become broader" as a result. Another consequence has been that decisions on larger project proposals can be made more quickly at the central level. In fact, this has been occurring if the project is in a priority area, and there are not other complexities associated with it.

The industrial and related reforms laid particular stress upon encouraging the high-tech electronics and communications industries. They also stimulated growth of industries to meet the demands for consumer durable products that are relatively easily available in the developed countries which so many middle-class Indians have visited or in which they have relatives. It was hoped too that as India expanded output of such products they might become internationally competitive in terms of price and quality, as occurred in the East Asian countries. These high- and medium-technology industries include the production of television sets and software, automobiles and commercial vehicles, other motor vehicles, and refrigerators, among other items. Excise taxes on such products were lowered; imports of machinery to produce them and of components for assembly were permitted; entry of firms into production of such items was eased, as

TABLE 2.
Output of some consumer durable goods in 1980–81 and 1987–88

Item	Output (in units, rounded)			
		1980/81		1987/88
Automobiles (cars, jeeps, and land-rovers)		50,000		171,000
Commercial vehicles		72,000		120,000
Motorcycles and scooters		450,000		1,500,000
Bicycles		4,000,000		6,700,000
Domestic refrigerators		290,000		680,000
Television sets	(1980)	85,000	(1986)	3,000,000

Sources: Tata Services, Statistical Outline of India, 1989–90 (Bombay, 1989), p. 73; televisions figure: CMIE, Production and Capacity Utilization in 600 Industries 1970–1986 (Bombay, 1987), pp. S-52 and S-54; Ninan, "Business and Economy," p. 42, estimates television production reached 6 million sets in the late 1980s.

was foreign investment and collaboration in their production. The result, in terms of the output of some of those goods, is shown in table 2.

The annual compound growth rate of output of consumer electronic products has been estimated at close to 40 percent from 1981 to 1987; of the professional electronics sector, which includes computers, at about 30 percent; and of components, the most important of which are electron tubes for television sets, at about 26 percent. The number of firms producing television sets grew from 89 in 1981 (86 of which were producing black and white sets) to 306 in 1987 (of which 133 were producing color sets); the number of firms producing computers grew from 8 to 118. (The rate of growth of India's total output of electronic goods in the 1980s exceeded that of South Korea from 1980 to 1985.)[48]

The above figures for the number of firms in consumer electronics may be limited to larger-scale firms, since the International Labor Organization estimated a total of 800 producing units in 1986. Many of these were in the small-scale industry sector, and the small units produced 58 percent of the 1987 value of output of consumer electronic products, and 38 percent of the value of the entire electronics output. Small units often "only [do] assembly work of . . . imported automated components. . . . The number of workers per unit [is] small as the system of subcontracting is very common."[49] While the average wage rate in the electronics industry as a whole doubled from 1981–82 to 1984–85, the wage rate for contract workers in the small units was about two-thirds that for regular workers in the large units; too, the number of engineers and technicians in small units is very low. Another significant trend in electronics, reflecting the increase in competition as more firms entered the industry, has been a general price decline for products. Prices of personal computers fell by over 80 percent from 1984 to 1986, but seem to have remained relatively stable since then. This stability after 1986 may reflect an apparent increase in the industry concentration ratio in 1987, compared to earlier years. There were also large increases in the number of producers of other types of consumer goods as well in the 1980s: the number of two-wheeler manufacturers rose from 6 to 15, of polyester yarn producers from 6 to 24, and of car manufacturers from 2 to 7.[50]

In addition to massive increases in the output of the electronics and various consumer durable industries, there have been marked increases in capacity and output between 1982 and 1986 for such housing-related products as cement, sanitary ware, and tiles, which benefited from greater demand for housing. The cement industry was also a particular beneficiary of reforms with respect to price and the compulsory allocation to government at a fixed price; the compulsory share was sharply reduced in 1982, freeing a greater share of output for sale at market price, and recently the fixed price share was abolished. The effect was very stimulating, cement capacity doubling from 26 million tons in 1980 to 52 million in 1986. Production also doubled from 18 million to 36 million tons, which contrasts with a rise in output of only 6 million tons for the entire 1970s decade. This rapid expansion was fueled by rising prices and the expectations of high profitability on the part of private businessmen. But as capacity grew, open-market cement prices began to fall, and profitability declined. "The industry then started the scare psychosis by proclaiming 'there is not enough demand for cement' in the country. The truth of the matter is there are no more long queues of consumers . . . waiting for their quota of cement. They can buy cement readily in the market at a price which may even be lower than the . . . controlled price. . . . [The] industry must lower its price, market its product, to create demand for cement rather than sit back and complain."[51]

Writing in late 1986, F. A. Mehta anticipated similar expansions of capacity in the private sector of the fertilizer industry as well as in the chemicals, motor vehicles, and electronics industries. This did occur and led to the disappearance of the supply shortages in those and other industries, and to the end of the black-market price premia that were common for those industries in which prices were controlled. Mehta anticipated that the massive investments made by the private corporate sector would lead to "conditions of glut with savage competition" in many industries. "[Thus] the logical result of a liberalized licensing policy is the promotion of competition."[52] In addition to expanding capacity there was significant private investment for the modernization of existing industrial plant. Modernization had lagged previously, reflecting low profitability, government control over expansion, and the guaranteed domestic market for output in short supply. "Major Indian industries presented a picture of obsolescence. . . . Since 1965–66 [there had been] an accumulated obsolescence in capital equipment, in technology and in skills." The reforms permitted modernization and expansion to optimum size in selected industries, and major programs in those directions were undertaken in the steel, cement, and textile industries.[53]

A large part of the funds required for investment in expansion and modernization was raised by private firms in the Indian stockmarkets, which now supplied 35–40 percent of the private sector's capital needs. The number of private companies listed on the stock exchanges almost tripled between 1981 and 1987, rising from 2,100 to 6,000. The total number of investors on the exchanges increased from 1 million in 1980 to 16 million in 1989; and with this great increase in activity the government introduced various institutional changes to better inform and safeguard the investor.[54]

As a result of the much greater competition within the private sector, the shift from a sellers' market to a buyers' market, and the falling prices and profits for uncompetitive firms, the problem of "industrial sickness" has become more serious than previously. A sick industrial unit is one that "has at the end of any financial year accumulated losses equal to or exceeding its entire net worth. . . ."[55] Bankruptcy in India is a very lengthy process that has not been encouraged. In the past the government nationalized some larger sick firms; it has not done so since 1983, but has set up financial institutions to assist them, and it provides a large amount of finance to them. The number of sick firms almost doubled from 1984 to 1987, increasing from 93,000 to 160,000. Of these 160,000 sick firms only 1,700 were large and medium-sized; the remainder were small-scale. Of the large sick firms about one-third were considered viable, another 40 percent clearly nonviable, with the remainder undetermined. Of the small firms fewer than 10 percent were considered viable. About half of all sick firms were in the engineering and textile industries, concentrated on the west coast in and near Bombay in Maharashtra state, and on the east coast in and near Calcutta. These two cities had been the historical centers of the cotton textile and jute industries, and of the older engineering industries (such as the manufac-

ture of railroad locomotives). These industries have been especially
hurt by the rise of new technologies in textiles and locomotion, by
foreign competition, and by India's own past policies. As of June 1987
over Rs. 57 billion (approximately $4.4 billion at the then Rs. 13/$1
exchange rate) was tied up in credit to all the sick units, of which Rs.
42 billion went to the large firms and Rs. 15 billion to the small ones.
(Of the total, Rs. 22 billion was for viable firms; about the same
amount to the clearly nonviable ones, and the remainder to the un-
derdetermined firms.)

    These policies to support sick firms reflect in part the political
significance of Maharashtra and West Bengal, and the power of the
trade unions in the engineering and textiles industries. But probably
more important is that there would be a serious unemployment problem if the sick enterprises in those industries closed. If we assume
roughly fifty workers per unit in the 1,700 larger sick firms, and ten
workers per unit in the 158,000 small units, we get a total of about 1.7
million workers employed in sick units (1.6 million in small ones and
100,000 in large ones), of whom 200,000 are in viable units. The total
of 1.7 million workers equals roughly one-third of the number of
workers in the entire private organized manufacturing sector (i.e.,
larger firms) in 1987, with those in smaller sick firms equal to about
15 percent of the more than 10 million workers in modern small-scale
industry. In the face of such numbers, and in light of any government's public commitment to reduce poverty and increase employment, there is understandably a great reluctance to allow firms to
fail, which would increase poverty and unemployment in the short
run. But the allocation of such a large amount of funds to support
firms, most of which are not viable, is a significant diversion of resources to nonproductive purposes, as well as an inflationary addition equal to 10 percent of the total bank credit outstanding in
mid-1987. There may be no alternative in the absence of an effective
unemployment compensation program, but it points up the strong
need for the government to develop an effective unemployment relief
and retraining/resettlement program. That would once more make
many of these workers productive economically, and would permit
the closing down of bankrupt enterprises.[56]

    While much of the deregulation and decontrol has been directed
toward the private sector, the reform process also sought to increase
efficiency and profitability of the public-sector enterprises. In fact relatively little has been achieved in developing MOUs to establish the
terms of an understanding between managers of centrally owned public enterprises and the central government. These were to spell out
the relations between the enterprise and the relevant government

agency it deals with, as well as present to the manager a set of mutually acceptable performance targets in terms of various criteria. In fact
only eleven such MOUs were signed between 1986 when this practice
was first introduced and May 1989; six more were in process of being
prepared. These obviously cover only a small percentage of the over
200 central public-sector enterprises, and their impact has been marginal.

A recent comparison of the profitability of public-sector firms
with a sample of large private firms over the 1973–74 to 1987–88
period shows an average gross rate of return on total capital of 10 percent for the public-sector firms and 23 percent for the private ones.
Not surprisingly the net profitability ratio (profit after taxes and interest on net worth) was 7 percent for the public firms and 12 percent
for the private firms over the same period. But these rates of return
have increased more rapidly in the public sector than in the private
one during this time. Many of these public-sector firms are profitable
less as a result of their competitive efficiency, and more because they
are monopolies and can sell their outputs at high administered prices.
The Seventh Five-Year Plan projected that the central government's
public sector enterprises would finance two-thirds of their investment requirements from internal sources. However during the first
three years of that plan they financed only one-third of their investment needs internally; the central government financed another 45
percent from its budget, and the remainder was funded from the securities market.[57]

Public-sector management reform efforts are directed toward
central government enterprises. Little consideration has been given
to the large state and local government enterprise sector, which in
1984–85 owned more factories, employed more workers, and had a
greater fixed investment in those plants than the central government
did in its plants. This state government sector had been growing
rapidly since 1977, largely for political reasons, in spite of the fact
that its "financial performance has been utterly dissatisfying. The total management performance is chaotic. The position with regard to
the internal generation of resources was dismal."[58] However the state
government plants have been largely ignored by the reform program,
essentially because they are the responsibility of the states, rather
than of the center.

While the effect of the reforms on public-sector performance in
the industrial sector has not been very significant in overall terms,
there has been a marked improvement in performance in infrastructure areas under government ownership such as power, transportation, and communication. This reflects both the large increase in

investment in that sector, and improvements in management and technology. Generated electric power grew at an annual rate of nearly 9 percent and almost doubled between 1980–81 and 1987–88, in large part because of the increase in coal production and the improved quality of coal from the government-owned coal-mining industry. The railroads were also able to ship this increased tonnage to the coal-fired power plants. The net effect was a marked improvement in the plant-load factor, especially for thermal power stations. This was of particular importance because the 1986–88 droughts had drastically reduced output of hydropower plants. Rail haulage of goods, which had increased by only 11 percent during the decade of the 1970s, grew by over 50 percent from 1980–81 to 1987–88. This resulted from better management but also from greater investment for rail equipment and line improvement. As a result of this improved performance the rail system raised its earnings by almost four times, thereby becoming less dependent on general budget funds for its investment needs and being able to finance far more of those requirements internally. There has also been greater investment in telecommunications, a marked raising of the technology level of that industry, and major institutional reforms in its operations. This contributed to some improvement in the performance of a notoriously inefficient industry. Several observers have concluded that the improvement in the performance of the infrastructure sector as a result of greater investment and better management has been a major factor behind the improved overall performance of the industrial sector in the 1980s.[59]

Another major area of reform has been the opening up of India to more foreign trade and investment. It was recognized that at least in the short run a significant increase in imports would be a necessary part of the process of raising India's level of technology and improving the quality of its output. As a counterpart to this, India's exports would also have to increase, perhaps at a slower pace, to avoid a serious debt problem. With the great increases in capacity and outputs for many industries, it was hoped that those industries would find markets overseas for some of their greater production.

Imports, which had been at an annual level of about $15 billion from 1980 to 1983, at first rose slowly reaching about $16–17 billion during the 1984–86 period, and then increased sharply to $19 billion in 1987 and again to $22 billion in 1988—or by almost 50 percent in the six years since 1983. Among the import groups the greatest increase was in capital goods, the rupee value of which approximately doubled between 1984–85 and 1987–88. There were also marked increases in imports of iron and steel products, of unprocessed gems for further processing and reexport, and of components for such consumer durables as electronics.[60]

The rise in capital goods imports has been explained in the 1987–88 *Economic Survey* as reflecting in part a "mismatch between supply and demand in the domestic market . . . for sophisticated and high precision machinery," in particular for machine tools and some items of electrical machinery. The survey also remarked on the "higher domestic prices vis-à-vis international prices" for capital goods.[61] With respect to steel imports, the domestic industry was unable to produce the special steels required for the new high-tech products entering production.[62]

I have already remarked on the rapid growth of India's electronics industry, a large importer of knocked-down components that are then assembled within the country. While component production has risen rapidly, it has lagged behind final output. This is explained by the fact that production of components is a relatively capital-intensive process compared to their assembly, and is therefore more difficult to enter. The value of imports as a percentage of India's production value of electronic goods rose from about one-third during the 1975–80 period to 45 percent in 1984–86. (This however is not unusual—in South Korea that ratio was 51 percent in 1980, falling to 41 percent in 1985.)[63] Imports too of unprocessed precious and semi-precious stones rose by over 250 percent in rupee terms from 1982–83 to 1987–88, but processed gems were also one of India's most rapidly rising classes of exports during the same period.[64]

India's exports also increased in the 1980s, in fact at a somewhat higher rate than imports in the latter part of that decade, but in lower absolute amounts. In 1980 they were at $8.5 billion, rose to $9.5 billion in 1982 and 1983, and then hovered between $9.5 and 10 billion until 1986. In 1987 there was a marked increase to $12 billion, followed by another increase to $14 billion in 1988. Major increases occurred in exports of such labor-intensive products as ready-made garments, leather goods, and gems and jewelry, all of which markedly increased their shares of total exports from 1983–84 to 1987–88. Exports of chemicals and machinery appear also to have increased their share in rupee terms but much less, if at all, in dollars. However despite those increases, India's total exports remain at below 1 percent of world exports, and at about 5–6 percent of its national income through the entire reform period.[65]

This is a comparatively modest performance in the trade field, certainly less than that of China, whose exports as a share of its GNP doubled from 1978 to 1988.[66] Among the several reasons given for In-

dia's modest performance in the export field are the higher production costs of Indian producers compared to their competitors. This
reflects India's "higher prices of importables or non-traded inputs
and . . . much lower levels of productivity; to some extent the origin
of both may lie in the failure to realize economies of scale."[67] Another
contributing factor is the "clearly lower profitability of exports compared to domestic sales. All the export incentives put together still
fall far short of the effective protection for import substitution."[68]
Unless profitability is equalized in both domestic and export markets
there will not be a "self-sustaining momentum . . . to Indian exports."[69] Past infrastructure shortages have clearly impinged on the
ability of Indian firms to meet deadlines on export performance. In
addition the inexperience of Indian producers in foreign markets
makes it difficult for them to compete in terms of the quality and service standards demanded by foreign buyers and supplied by competitors. Such standards were rarely demanded by domestic buyers who
had no alternative suppliers.

With India's imports rising in absolute terms by a greater amount
than its exports, India's annual deficit on its foreign trade account increased by about $7 billion from 1985 to 1988. While invisible earn-
ings offset from 55 to 70 percent of the trade deficit during the Sixth-
Plan Period (1980–85), invisibles offset less than 40 percent of the
trade deficits in the years since 1985. This is in part explained by
rising interest payments on foreign debt since 1985, which counterbalanced more of such earnings. The result has been a doubling of foreign debt between 1984 and 1989, and a steady decline in the
country's foreign exchange reserves, which had fallen to a level of six
weeks of imports by September 1989. India's debt service ratio grew
from 8 percent to more than 30 percent over the same period. That
latter ratio is above the 20 percent ratio that the world financial community normally considers safe.[70]

There has been some increase in annual direct foreign investment in India. In 1981 it was only $14 million, rose to about $50 million in 1983, and then increased to over $100 million per year from
1984 to 1987, before reaching about $120 million in 1988 (Ninan
gives a figure of $170 million for 1988). There have been substantial
investments by German, United States, British, and Japanese companies among others. But while this is a turnaround from the divest-
ment of the 1970s, these levels are still "modest by world standards."
Direct foreign investment in India totaled about $500 million from
1981 to 1987. Over the same period Singapore, Taiwan, and Thailand
each received about $4 billion of direct foreign investment; China,

from 1980 to 1988, and Indonesia, from 1981 to 1987, each received on the order of $9 billion.[71]

With the increase in foreign direct investment there has been a doubling in the number of approved collaborations between Indian and foreign firms. These grew from about 500 in 1980 to 1,000 per year in 1985 and thereafter. While this is still a relatively low figure by world standards, such collaborations have contributed to the modernization that I remarked upon in Indian industry. However their impact on India's industry as a whole remains marginal.

Ashok Desai has pointed out that a major constraint on the export of technology to India and the willingness of foreign firms to collaborate with Indian firms is that Indian markets for many technology items are simply too small to be profitable. Furthermore India's own technology import policies, which keep down the prices that Indian firms can pay for technology, while restricting access of foreign firms to India's domestic market for sale of their products, discourage foreign firms from supplying their technology to Indian firms. This is quite apart from the entire regulatory structure of industry with its lengthy bureaucratic procedures for foreign entry, which have discouraged potential foreign technology suppliers and collaborators in the past. The reforms have chipped away at these constraints but only in part.[72]

What were the overall economic results of this reform period? Ninan notes that after Rajiv Gandhi's accelerated reform program began in 1985 the economy grew from 1985 to 1988–89 at an annual rate of "nearly 5.5 percent."[73] This was despite two bad drought years, 1986–87 and 1987–88, during which agricultural output fell by almost 3.0 percent per year, and food-grains output by almost 4.5 percent per year. But industrial output, somewhat unusually, rose by over 8 percent in each of those drought years, which indicates that the weather and agricultural output are no longer the governing factors for the performance of the economy as a whole or of industry. And in 1988–89, with the return of good weather, it appears on the basis of preliminary figures that agricultural production grew on the order of 15 percent or more as it caught up with the predrought trend. Industrial output grew by almost 9 percent and national income by 9 percent. (Per capita income grew at about 3.2 percent during the entire 1985–89 period, and at a 6.9 percent rate in the final year, 1988–89.)[74] These accelerated growth rates of gross national product or national income in the latter half of the decade appeared to confirm India's breakthrough to a level beyond the 3.5 percent "Hindu rate of growth" barrier of the previous decades.

With respect to industrial growth per se there is agreement of a rising overall growth rate in the decade of the 1980s, regardless of the base period used for the index of industrial production. Using a revised 1980–81 base, the index shows a rise to an annual rate of 7.2 percent from 1981 to 1986. This is a higher annual growth rate than the 5.6 percent rate for the entire 1951–86 period or the 5.0 percent rate for the decade of the 1970s, or in fact for any previous decade. The previously used 1970–71 based index also shows a rise, but to a 6.3 percent annual rate in the 1980s. This however also exceeds the 5.1 percent growth rate, using that base, for the entire 1951–86 period, as well as the rate for the decade of the 1970s, and in fact for any previous decade.[75] (There has been some controversy among economists as to whether the change in the base led to an exaggeration of the real industrial growth rate.) Further research using National Accounts Statistics (NAS) would appear to confirm this acceleration in the industrial growth rate in the 1980s compared to the period 1966–67 to 1978–79, and it may even exceed the high growth rates of the early 1960s. According to the same national accounts data the growth rate in output of registered manufacturing (i.e., large and medium-sized firms) was over 10 percent per year in the 1980s compared to the overall rate of growth in all manufacturing of over 8 percent, indicating that large- and medium-scale manufacturing grew more rapidly than the small-scale sector. The two most rapidly growing subsectors of manufacturing were consumer durables and capital goods production.[76] As noted earlier the effect of this growth was to end the shortage situation and psychology that had earlier characterized industry.

However in 1989–90 there seems to have been a decline in the rate of growth of GNP and manufacturing output compared to the previous very high annual rates. GNP, which was estimated to have risen by about 10 percent in the previous year, rose by only about 4.5 percent in 1989–90. (This in part reflected a return to the normal rate of agricultural growth after the record rise in 1988–89.) But more relevant for our analysis is the sharply declining rate of growth of the manufacturing index, which fell from a 10 percent rate in April–November 1988, to a 3.6 percent rate for the same period in 1989. A major element in this overall decline was the fall in the growth rate of consumer durable production from 19 percent in 1988 to less than 1 percent in 1989. Associated with this was a lesser reduction in growth rates for the basic and intermediate goods sectors. Unfortunately the *Economic Survey* for 1989–90 provides no analysis of the factors behind this sharp fall in the growth rate of consumer durables output. One hypothesis was that there had been a saturation of demand for such goods in the upper-middle-income groups who were the main buyers during the previous few years. The effect of this mid-1989 decline was a fall in the overall growth rate for industry to less than 6.0 percent in 1989–90, well below the 8.0 percent target. However agricultural outputs continued to increase to record totals in 1990, and this contributed to an annual growth rate of 12 percent for industrial output during the first six months of FY 1990–91 (i.e., April 1 to September 30, 1990). However after the Persian Gulf crisis began in August 1990, that industrial growth rate is estimated to have declined to about 7 percent for the remainder of the year.[77]

One of the hoped-for results from the accelerated industrial growth rate was an increase in industrial employment that would begin to change the country's employment structure. "Data on employment . . . are scarce, in some cases non-existent, and in all cases discontinuous, and have to be derived from various sources. . . . The result is that they are sometimes contradictory and cannot be reconciled."[78] But there does seem to be agreement that the increase in employment in industry during the period since 1985 has been small. Abid Hussain, a member of the Planning Commission during Rajiv Gandhi's period as prime minister (from 1985 to late 1989) concludes that "the rate of new job creation in the organized sector of industry has not kept pace with requirements. In the organized manufacturing sector as a whole, employment elasticity with respect to output has declined [markedly] from . . . the 1970s to . . . the 1980s."[79] There has been a higher figure for the employment elasticity in the unorganized segment of manufacturing industry, but the total employment effect remains low. Adiseshiah, after examining various data, concludes that at the end of the Seventh Plan, "there will be . . . an unemployed backlog of about the same number as at the start."[80] Various bits of data do indicate a low rate of growth of organized sector employment in the period of the Seventh Plan, well below the rate of entry of new workers in the labor force. Private-sector organized manufacturing employment at best stayed constant if it did not actually decline, while public-sector manufacturing may have increased by several hundred thousand. There may have been an increase of 1 million workers in the small-scale manufacturing sector from 1985 to 1987. With such low employment growth it is not surprising that Hussain speaks of the need for a "change in the policies that bias growth towards higher capital intensity . . . policies that reduce the cost of capital [and] . . . that raise the effective cost of labour."[81] With such marginal effects on employment one would not expect much impact toward the reduction of poverty, although recent data are lacking on this matter.

There are certain significant problem areas associated with the reform process itself. I have already remarked that changes in public-sector enterprise management have been marginal, and that most such enterprises have not been granted much more autonomy than in the past. With respect to the private sector, Ninan notes that "this is not a free business environment, but one with open and hidden strings for control by the government. And invariably, the most successful business executives . . . are the ones with the best connections in New Delhi." "In one way or another," he continues, "officials manage to position themselves and retain enough discretionary control to ensure that businessmen have to keep going to them as supplicants. The experience of Indian businessmen has been that while controls seemingly have been relaxed . . . the need to refer things to government remains."[82] In the first years of Rajiv Gandhi's leadership his office apparently exerted enough pressure upon the bureaucracy to speed the decision-making process, especially in areas of top priority. But as the honeymoon ended, with growing political difficulties and with charges of corruption even reaching to the circle around the prime minister, less pressure could be exerted upon the bureaucracy, and old party members with connections with businessmen were once again brought back into influential positions. Too, new brooms in the central government had far less impact on the state governments, which had their own requirements and permissions, to be met or circumvented by one means or another. Thus business-political connections remained close, and payoffs in exchange for approvals of one's own requests, or even disapprovals of those of competitors, were considered normal.

Regional issues remained important despite the industrial reform program. Many of the exemptions from licensing provisions, especially for larger firms, were contingent upon construction of the new plant in an industrially backward area. Thus while the number of industrial licenses issued declined significantly as more of the smaller enterprises were exempt, of the licenses issued the proportion for the backward areas rose from 30 percent of the total from 1980 to 1984, to about 40–45 percent from 1985 to 1989.[83] Such plants might be profitable within India because their newer technologies could compensate for the higher costs of a poorer location that might lack adequate transport, power, and social infrastructure, but this would be less likely in the world markets. This regional dispersion of industry is considered to be a major factor contributing to India's difficulties in expanding its exports, especially of engineering products.

India's worsening foreign balance-of-payments position, in spite of a more rapid rate of growth of exports than of imports in recent years, has intensified the pressures to again tighten controls on imports. Such pressures are supported not only as a short-term expedient to deal with a foreign-exchange problem, but also on nationalist grounds to reduce the threat of imports of capital goods to India's own capital goods industry. There are also anticonsumerism arguments that component imports for consumer electronics and other durables are unnecessary for the building up of the economy, while pandering to middle-class, foreign-influenced tastes. However reintroducing tight controls on such imports would have a strong negative impact on India's efforts to modernize its own heavy industries and to expand its exports of engineering and high-tech products, as well as on the two fastest growing segments of its manufacturing sector—consumer durables and capital goods. It has been estimated that "the average Indian industrial product tends to cost twice as much as its equivalent abroad while consumer electronics goods cost two to three times world levels."[84] Tightening import controls might well, in the short run, widen rather than reduce these differences.

An important issue related to the reforms is that they probably have had minor benefits for lower-income sectors of the economy and society. The industrial employment effects have apparently been significantly less than hoped for in the Seventh Five-Year Plan; the reduction of poverty has probably been marginal. The reforms have been criticized for contributing to greater inequality of incomes within India by reducing direct income taxes, by the sale of tax-free, high-interest-yielding securities to upper-income buyers, and by reducing excise taxes on durable consumer goods "which cater to the rich and the upper middle classes."[85] At the same time the spread of television sets throughout India has made the difference between the life-styles of the high- and middle-income classes and those of the urban and rural poor more obvious to the latter. V. K. R. V. Rao notes that "the [increase in] income inequalities . . . is being brought to the public view by the TV network. . . . This inequality is not only at the top most levels but also in middle class levels."[86] It extends also between workers in the organized sector of industry, whether public or private, and those in the unorganized industrial and agricultural sectors, not only with respect to wages but also to all types of nonwage benefits—insurance, retirement provisions, holidays, and others.[87]

India's higher growth rates since the early 1980s have also been accompanied by a steady rise in the consumer price index on the order of 8–10 percent per year from 1984–85 to 1987–88. This has been fueled by an annual rise in the money supply on the order of 10–20 percent per year over the same period.[88] That rise largely reflects increased borrowing by the central government from the Reserve Bank of India and other banks to finance a steadily increasing deficit.

The Chakravarty Committee Report of 1985, presented just after Rajiv Gandhi's election as prime minister, highlighted some of the key
issues associated with deficit financing, which have in fact become
sharper since then. It points out that there was a major rise in India's
savings rate between the early 1950s and the 1980s. Despite this,
"government has been incurring deficits which suggests that its access to savings falls short of its expenditures and is not keeping pace
with the growing demands on government which are reflected in the
rising volume of subsidies, buffer stock operations, as also developmental expenditures. . . . [The] rising quantum of interest payments
on a growing volume of domestic borrowings have also contributed to
the sharp increase in current expenditures over the two years while
current revenues have not shown the same degree of buoyancy. The
revenue account of the combined budgets of the Central and State
governments reveals sizeable deficits since 1982–83, instead of [the
earlier] surplus."[89] The report warned against unduly large deficit financing via credit from the Reserve Bank of India, and urged action to
tap savings to a greater degree than in the past, to raise savings of public enterprises, and to lower costs of government by improving government efficiency.[90]

Tax revenues did increase after 1985, but current expenditures
rose at an even faster rate, especially for increasing interest payments
on the growing debt, for defense, and for ongoing costs of government
as these rose with rising prices. The government was not able to
find new sources of revenue—one obvious source would have been
a central income tax on farm incomes, but this was politically impossible though economists had recommended such a tax for some
time. One area in which government investment has been adversely
affected by the continuing deficit is agriculture, "especially in irrigation [the consequences of which] will be felt for many years to
come."[91]

One is struck, in looking at the Indian fiscal experience of the past
decade, with its similarities to the United States since 1980: problems of budget deficits and trade deficits, savings lags and difficulties
in raising taxes, and the delaying of useful public investment. Some of
the political issues in changing policies in India also resemble those
in the United Stats. While the Reserve Bank of India does not have the
independence from the Treasury that the Federal Reserve Board has,
the conservative policies of the RBI have played a major role in controlling India's annual inflation rate within a range of 5–10 percent
since 1984. It is also probable that this deficit financing, and steady
price rise, for which organized sector employees have been compen-
sated by rising wages, have had a stimulating effect on business ex-

pectations and industrial performance since 1985, upon the boom in the securities markets, and upon the rising demand for consumer durable goods which have been so important in stimulating industry. Over this same period too the exchange value of the rupee has been allowed to depreciate in line with the overall trend of rising prices, and this has reduced any negative effect of the price rise upon exports.[92] But those many groups in society who either did not gain directly from the higher prices as businessmen do, or who did not have the political or economic strength to compel action by their employers or the state to compensate for the price rises, suffered as a result. This contributed to the apparent widening of the income disparities within Indian society that Rao remarked upon. Those inequalities, of which people have become more conscious than in the past, together with the greater corruption at all levels in society, contributed to the defeat of Rajiv Gandhi and the Congress party in the elections of late 1989, in spite of the apparently booming economy.

CONTRASTING EFFECTS OF THE REFORMS IN CHINA AND INDIA

In both China and India the economic reforms contributed to higher rates of overall economic growth, and higher rates of industrial growth in particular in the 1980s. The Chinese results however were greater than in India in terms of both those measures of performance. This may well reflect the very positive improvements in agricultural production and incomes as a result of China's initial reform giving households control over farm decisions. India had no such sharp improvement in agricultural incomes to provide a major stimulus to industrial demand; rather the demand that fueled India's increasing output was a demand for consumer durables on the part of the large numbers of people in the top quintile of the income distribution. This was clearly a more narrow population base for the reforms to build on than in China. But this in turn reflected the fact that India's agricultural system and policies had remained largely stable since the late 1960s, while China's farm sector had gone through several dramatic shifts in organization and policy—the latest reform was such a shift, but with strong positive results.

The stimulating change in China's farm system was accompanied by a separate policy shift that delegated to local and provincial governments both significant economic powers and a large share of the revenues derived from effective use of those powers. This contributed to an especially sharp increase in the numbers and output of

rural-based, locally owned industrial enterprises, whether cooperatively or privately owned. There was also a very large increase in industrial employment in rural areas. Nothing similar to this occurred
in India, in part because there was no jump in farm incomes, but perhaps more important, because there was no such delegation of economic power and resources to local agencies. India's reform eased the
entry of large-scale enterprises into backward economic areas, but
the effects on employment in rural-based industry were apparently
slight.

China's economic reforms also had far more positive results in
encouraging foreign trade and investment by foreign enterprises than
did India's. In part this reflected the close connections between the
PRC and Hong Kong, which served as a major conduit for flows of
goods and capital into and out of China. But the ability to take advantage of Hong Kong's presence arose from reforms that changed the
foreign-trade system from one of detailed central control to one that
encouraged and rewarded local and enterprise trade initiatives. Indian
reforms in effect relaxed some of the earlier restrictions on trade
and foreign investment, but the system still remained a complex and
restrictive one. Indian firms too lacked foreign-trade experience
and even after the reforms found the partially protected domestic
market more profitable than the highly competitive international
market. But both countries, as trade increased, found imports rising
more rapidly than exports, with consequently growing balance-of-
payments deficits and foreign debt, the latter a greater problem for India. And in both countries, despite the opening of their economies,
there are strong nationalist pressures to restrict imports and direct
investment by foreigners other than overseas and Hong Kong Chinese
in the case of China, and nonresident Indians in India's case.

In both countries too there are strong regional pressures to set up
industries in "backward" and economically less-developed areas.
These arise from strong regional political elements, reflecting in India's case ethnic and linguistic differences which are greater than in
China, but in both countries supported by security considerations. In
China such regional dispersion has had very significant positive
effects on employment, but in both countries it has led to the setting
up of uneconomic enterprises possibly isolated from larger markets
by distance or uneconomic size. Because of the political connections
it becomes difficult to close down such enterprises or allow them to
fail.

Apart from geographic issues, in both countries many of the
public-sector enterprises are consistent loss-makers that cannot be

shut down and are therefore continuously subsidized from central or state budgets, or by bank credits. Neither country has an effective unemployment relief and training system, so in effect the maintaining of such enterprises performs this function. There are also strong political pressures, worker expectations, and ideological pressures that make bankruptcy and closure of even continuously losing firms very difficult.

Part of the Chinese reform program has been to set up various institutions that India already has. These include a body of contract laws and courts to adjudicate disputes, a securities market, encouraging within limits a private sector especially for services, and an educational system to train highly skilled technical and professional workers. Much of China's higher educational system was destroyed during the Cultural Revolution and has had to be rebuilt. In India these various institutions, including the education system, already exist and operate—the issue is more to improve their functioning, and/or make them available to a wider public.

Both countries have had significant macroeconomic problems associated with their reforms. In China the devolution of financial powers and resources to localities to carry out their own investment programs, together with the expansion of a banking system closely associated with local political leadership, has contributed to periodic surges in credit to finance local and provincial investment. This has been associated with increases in bank-financed debt and in currency. There is no effective macrocontrol system, so that the consequence has been upward price surges then curbed by central government crash financial control programs. There have been several such cycles in the 1978–89 period, and the lack of control over them has set limits on the extent of the economic reforms and contributed to political unrest. India on the contrary has an effective macrocontrol system. This has moderated price rises and contributed to a steady, but relatively low rate of inflation—and probably also to a psychological climate conducive to rising business expectations. But India has not succeeded in curbing the central government's own financial deficit, arising from pressures for subsidies from politically powerful demand groups, greater defence spending, and rising interest expenditures, combined with tax revenues that are difficult to raise and low public-enterprise profits. (India in these respects may resemble the United States more than it does China). This deficit, financed by Central Bank credit and rising currency supplies, has fueled inflation at the same time that funds for economically productive government expenditures have been reduced. Nor has the Indian government been able to compensate for the negative effects of this steady, even if relatively low, rate of price rise upon the great bulk of the population that does not have the political strength to protect its real income.

In China, the combination of the rising prices and the newly introduced dual-price system for many products, with widening inflation-induced differences between the set price and the rising market price for a particular item, has contributed to growing corruption. Formerly this had been limited by legal restrictions and ideological beliefs, but both of these were relaxed as a product both of the process of introducing the reforms, and of the weakening of the felt ideological restraints. The growing inequalities and spreading corruption associated with higher prices contributed to the widespread public dissatisfaction that led to open political unrest, culminating in the Tiananmen Square violence of June 1989.

In India, corruption had long been associated with the complex regulatory system. The reforms, while relaxing the regulatory controls, did not face up to the problem of corruption, which in fact seemed to have increased and was believed to have reached higher levels of the government after 1984. This contributed to growing dissatisfaction with Rajiv Gandhi's government, and was an important factor in its defeat in the November 1989 elections.

CHAPTER FIVE

Economic Reform and Political Systems

Max Planck said that a science progresses by having the old professors die off.

GEORGE J. STIGLER, *Memoirs of an Unregulated Economist*

Then it's moved and seconded that the compulsory retirement age be advanced to ninety-five.

Caption to a PETER ARNO cartoon

C HAPTER 1 presented various major elements of the political economies of China and India. This chapter will explore how the economic reforms in each country interacted with the political-economic systems of each, and the implications of that interaction for the future of each country's economic reforms and political system.

CHINA

Mao, at his death, left China firmly under the rule of the Communist party, but there was disagreement among his successors as to the future path of policy. There was a minority in the party that believed on ideological grounds that China had still not approached true communism and that this direction should be pushed. But this minority was soon eliminated with the arrest of the "Gang of Four." The top leaders who inherited power or gradually came to power agreed that China must modernize under the leadership of the party. There was disagreement as to the pace of that modernization process and its relationship to China's recent history. Here again Hua Guofeng, who advocated very rapid growth policies *and* adherence to Mao's ideology and prescriptions, was criticized for failing in his economic policies.

He was forced out by Deng Xiaoping and his allies, who agreed on both the need for modernization and an approach that relied less on ideology and more on experiment and practice, but under the leadership of a reformed party. There was still disagreement among the new leaders on the pace of modernization and the relationship between Communist theory and practice on such economic issues as planning versus the market, but all the new leaders had been under attack and exiled from power during the Cultural Revolution, and they agreed on the urgency of economic improvement for the country.

This demand for economic improvement had a much deeper base in Chinese society. For the approximately twenty years before Mao's death there had been little if any improvement in the individual well-being of the Chinese worker or farmer, in spite of the rise of a large industrial base. At the same time the persecutions and shifting policies and conflicts of the Cultural Revolution years undermined belief in the party's leadership and ideas.

Yves Chevrier argues that "Maoism did achieve party domination of the whole [of Chinese society] . . . through economic as well as political means. . . . [But] it proved unable to achieve the other goal of communism: that of economic growth and country-strengthening which goes beyond mere party building. . . . [In fact the Maoist policy] had been built at the expense of modernization."[1] This failure of Maoism to establish the basis for a "rich and strong country" led to "a tremendous sense of loss" and frustration. This wider frustration underlay the priority placed upon economic improvement by the party leaders after 1978.

How was this demand for economic reform and modernization implemented by the new leaders within the framework of the party system left by Mao? Even after Deng's victory over Hua, significant differences remained among the party leaders, on such specific issues as the appropriate degree of economic modernization, the speed of the process, and the correct areas of policy change in relation to both the maintenance of a socialist society and the position of the party. The implementation of the reform process would have to take these differences into account; it was hoped that successes in achieving particular ends would maintain agreements among the leaders to go on to the next stage.

A general overview shows that the Chinese reforms and their socio-economic consequences grew by fitting in with the environment, thanks to the concurring acceptance by the system (established power networks and social interests) of certain structural changes up to certain levels. In other words, the mutual acceptance of system and reforms rested on a double basis, one general, one specific. The first [general] basis was the post-Mao decision to retreat from the all-out command approach of Stalinism and Maoism. This allowed social pluralism and ideological withdrawal within the formerly non-economic sphere of economic organization. The second, more specific, basis amounted to a secondary, or complementary, legitimacy for reforms, built around three main pillars: 1) economic performance and expediency; 2) the appeal to private and group interests within and without the power structure; and 3) the relative harmlessness of the reforms and their consequences to the overall balance of the system. . . .

A few rules of thumb seem to emerge from the Chinese practice beyond the decentralized and trial and error process . . . readily admitted by the Chinese authorities. . . . The basic rule is that, as in guerrilla warfare, reforms advance more where there is more space for them in the political and organizational web of the system. They also take advantage of social support from various segments, avoiding—or retreating from—areas where there is more resistance and/or no support. A second rule, then, becomes apparent. In a mosaic-like, continent-size country, with low state and economic integration, good reforms are divided reforms. The decentralized and marginal approach—exemplified, for instance, in the special status granted to Guangdong or in the relative advance of rural reforms after 1980—had a structural edge over the centralized and urban orientation of the USSR and Eastern European satellites, at least so long as cumulative economic effects did not overflow the urban core (which had happened in 1985), and as long as the centrifugal organizational effects inherent in the structural avoidance process did not threaten party and country unity (a threat also felt in 1985).[2]

The salient feature of the earliest reform after Mao's death was that it occurred in the rural area. Among the reasons for that was "the loose geography of China's bureaucratic integration [which permitted] factional politics [to become] oppositional provincial policies." The rural reforms could thus be introduced in provinces such as Sichuan and Anhui, where they proved their success, in spite of the fact that in Beijing, Hua still pressed for old Maoist policies. But these reforms did not threaten party rule even though their success weakened one leadership faction. This was, in Chevrier's words, because "a peasant society is a fragmented body, not an integrated whole able to . . . challenge state power. The peasants could thus push forward without endangering the overall political balance of the system. . . . Rural voices need intercessors to be heard at the higher levels. They cannot aggregate in power networks able to bear on interest groups and factional struggles at the top. . . . [Local] leaders do not count in the established political society which runs the pre-modern command structure." Thus "the communal dynamism of rural society and the erosion of party power in the villages, as well as the marginal position of the countryside in the distribution of *actual* power" made it possible to introduce reform in the rural area first, and contributed to the success of those rural reforms. This success set the groundwork for attempts at urban reform.

But urban reform is politically more difficult for the party, because urban society is an "integrated whole" which can "negotiate with or . . . challenge state power. . . . [Thus] a communist system . . . must not just control, but conquer" urban society. The conventional communist system controls urban society through "centrally controlled networks anchored in heavy industry and large scale projects." The reforms were first introduced in the less integrated sectors of the urban economy such as smaller enterprises, retail trade and marketing, and services. Reforms in these sectors "reduce but do not disconstruct centrally controlled networks anchored in heavy industry and large-scale projects." And thus they remain broadly compatible with the demands of the leaders who prefer to go slowly on the reforms, both on ideological grounds that socialism should control the commanding heights of the economy, with planning an integral part of that control, and on the grounds that rapid reform might destabilize the economy, as it did under Mao and Hua. Thus "while many enterprises, some goods and some areas have been granted a certain measure of freedom, many still remain under direct central control."

"[The] Chinese economy has become more economic, and controls less direct. . . . [But] non-political macro-economic regulation, still in its incipient phase . . . is in jeopardy because of weak central state control over the regulators (taxes, [money supply], credit, wages) rather than sheer lack of market information. . . . [The] guerrilla principle (good reforms are divided reforms) has allowed the encirclement of the urban fortress. The obvious failure of this approach, however, is that the growth of a reformed urban sector tends to erode the system further while reforms are not allowed to go far enough to give a decisive start to a new kind of integration."

In fact Chevrier remarks that the reform process has led to "acute economic and social imbalances"—regional and sectoral imbalances; a "renewed ascendancy of interpersonal relations"; and the generation of "genuine class tensions" as urban workers and students lose because their wages and benefits lag behind inflation, and the large number of migrants to the cities who are not "integrated in the

[work unit] safety net . . . [confront] the new wealth of the countryside and bureaucratic profiteering."

"While workers have [opposed the reforms] . . . (by pushing
wages and bonuses higher and resisting new rules and standards of
discipline and productivity), party, state and military cadres, at all
levels, have not displayed [an] overall resistance to reform." The state
and party officials kept their high position in the system because the
planning principle was retained, while at the same time they could
turn "to profitable activities in the new sphere of commodity economy. . . . [The] economic opportunities of the bureaucracy have been
extended far beyond the former black market activities. The Chinese
reforms owe much to their indirect appeal to bureaucratic interests
and to the . . . fact that the . . . decentralizing process gave more
room to local power networks" to which factory heads must conform.
This also leads to corruption, which is "the price to pay for divided
reforms" reflecting "the horizontal, centrifugal strength of the communities (structured by kinship and *guanxi*) as opposed to the . . .
weakness of the vertical state."

Chevrier goes on to argue that the post-Mao reforms have started
China on the path to modernization, which in his opinion is the
building of a modern state closely integrated with society. What Mao
built was a party system controlling a state based upon historical
communal and kinship factors interlinked with the party. In that
state there are "recurrent interventions from above . . . [but] never
sustained enough to give a decisive . . . edge to the state against communal entropy. . . . [Post-Mao] China must build the state more at
the expense of the traditional communal pattern. In this light the . . .
strategy of . . . Chinese modernization . . . becomes clearer: a more
modern economy, based on individual contractual relationships, demands a better integrated society based on educated and disciplined
entities." In the economic sphere, in addition to the above-
mentioned directions, the strategy calls for moving the social protection system "from the state as communities (enterprises) . . . to the
state as state." It also requires the introduction of an effective macroeconomic regulatory system, as opposed to the present political
control system with power alternating between the center and the local community.

"The post-Mao transition to modernization—that is from system building to state building depends on . . . active and independent
private family members, consumers and taxpayers as workers, peasants, entrepreneurs, writers, artists, experts, officials; [but also as] dependent and submissive citizens."

Obvious questions are whether such a combination of active and independent family members and workers *and* submissive citizens is politically feasible and what its effect would be upon the party system. Chevrier asks, "What if the statecraft of modernization keeps the new economy but . . . transforms some of the players? What if . . . the new state-society integration, however authoritarian, does not respect the privileged status of the party and its ideological monopoly?" Answering on the basis of the 1978–85 experience, Chevrier feels that "these contradictions can be resolved, with tactical flexibility and some delay." In the light of the experiences of the period from 1985 to 1989 it is difficult to be as optimistic. Local decentralization of economic decision-making became even stronger, the macroeconomic variables—money supply and credit investment, wages and consumption—moved further out of control, inflationary pressures became much stronger, and prices shot up, as did urban panic, perceived corruption, and perceived inequities among groups. The political reforms in Eastern Europe and an awareness through radio and television of student demonstrations for a more democratic system in some neighboring countries contributed to an urban protest movement, which was regarded as a threat to the system by the party leaders, and was crushed in Beijing by bringing in the army. That experience, if anything, supports Chevrier's earlier argument that a Communist system cannot live with an integrated urban society that it has not conquered.

Two possible economic policy directions within the present party system are, first, the establishment of an effective system to control the sharp fluctuations of macroeconomic variables, thus permitting introduction of wider price and market reforms and greater autonomy for enterprise managers. The second is the replacement of the present "iron rice bowl" work-unit-supplied social safety net by a state social welfare program, thus moving away from regarding the enterprise work unit as a guarantor of employment and minimal social well-being. But it is very doubtful that the party system, as it functions at present, can move in either direction in the near future. China lacks knowledge and experience in both areas. Apart from that there would be strong opposition to those steps for both ideological and bureaucratic reasons. Further loosening of microcontrols and the communal safety net would be regarded by some leaders as an ideological retreat from socialism and planning of key sectors. It would also eliminate the gains to party officials from the present system of microcontrols and political connections with the banking system, and would raise a fear of unemployment among workers. Without those institutions and policies, however, sharp economic fluctuations and inflations are to be expected in the future that will require strong central interventions into the economy. The possibilities for a consistent long-range improvement in overall economic performance will be limited. These swings may in turn lead to periodic political crises arising from public reaction to economic difficulties.

Dong Fureng, one of China's foremost economists, has written on the need for greater public discussion leading to better understanding of issues of economic reform and the difficulties of reform. In his opinion party and government officials must both share and be seen as sharing the difficulties that might accompany such reforms. If such broader discussions and the sharing of difficulties are regarded as threats to the party's present leadership and monopoly of power, and to the perquisites of party power, as they were in June 1989, they are very unlikely to occur, so long as the leadership is unchanged, and thus the entire future of economic reform is constrained. If however such broader discourse does in fact occur, what will be the future of the party's leadership position? In Chevrier's terms, is the system introduced by Mao and modified by Deng compatible with the conditions required for modernization of the Chinese state and society? It is this conflict between the system and requirements for modernization that sets the limits to urban economic reform. It is quite possible that these limits have been reached under the present party leadership with respect to major areas of policy in which further economic reform is necessary.

INDIA

Unlike China, India neither suffered the shock of a Cultural Revolution to create a major political push for reform, nor had a lagging rural economy to provide an initial area of reform from which broad substantial gains in output and income were quickly possible, thus stimulating reform in other sectors of the economy. Rather Indira Gandhi was reelected after having been out of power for several years, and there was a political need to appeal to other groups in society than those to which she had heretofore appealed. In addition there was an awareness that Indian industry was lagging in taking advantage of new technologies, and that opportunities existed for developing such durable goods industries as television. Meeting popular demands for such products would have some advantageous political benefits. The reforms were begun by Mrs. Gandhi modestly and peripherally, and they had modest positive results as far as the economy was concerned. They were essentially technical reforms drawing on reports of expert committees that were established to examine the need for policy changes in various sectors of the economy and to recommend appropriate changes. Some of the suggestions were introduced, especially in the areas of technology catch-up and export promotion, by modifying existing regulations and introducing new ones. The approach was low-keyed and very piecemeal and operated within the existing regulatory and ideological system.

Under Rajiv Gandhi the reforms were accelerated, and in various speeches he spoke forcefully on the need for reforms. But other than the Seventh Plan document, there was never any white paper that presented an overall argument for economic reform and placed specific reforms within the broader context of the Indian economy, society, and polity. Nor were the hoped-for benefits of the industrial reforms ever developed and presented in terms of their desired impact on other sectors of the society, or of how that wider impact was to be achieved. Some of that narrowness and marginality was deliberate, undoubtedly reflecting a fear on the part of the prime minister of arousing antagonism to, and within, the Congress party. But the result was that the reforms were seen as a collection of piecemeal attempts to modify the existing system of controls over industry, finance, and taxation in order to achieve very specific goals. As such, once Rajiv Gandhi's electoral honeymoon was over, they were regarded as specific changes affecting specific industries and groups, subject to being whittled away or expanded in response to specific pressures. (It resembles the American process of changes in a complex tax bill that lends itself to endless bargaining over specific provisions affecting specific groups that might benefit or lose.) What was sacrificed was an appeal to a broader public who might understand what was being done for the wider public good, and who would strengthen the ability of the groups pushing the reforms to prevent their being whittled down by vested interests.

It was also never explained how the reforms fit within the broad ideology of India's "socialistic pattern of society." (Again in an American comparison, the United States regards itself as a capitalist society. Legislation that is painted as socialist lends itself to attack, and proposals to enlarge the role of government must be justified as contributing to the better functioning of capitalism.) The compatibility of reform of India's industrial control system with the better functioning of a socialist society was never made clear, nor was the fact that many intellectuals believing in socialism considered the existing regulatory system both inefficient and corrupt. Nor was the relationship of the essentially urban industrial reforms to such broader socialist goals as reducing poverty, or raising rural incomes and outputs, or achieving a better life for all Indians ever articulated. As a result the specific reforms never had a wide public support among the large majority of the people who initially favored the general idea of reform, but who saw the benefits of particular reforms as at best tangential to their own interests, if not directly harmful, as they were at times painted by opponents on grounds of interest or ideology.

Some economists argued strongly for such a head-on approach to the reform issue. But a more cautious judgment prevailed, especially after Rajiv Gandhi was unsuccessful in persuading the party itself to support the reforms unequivocally. Many political figures saw the "socialist" pattern of Indian society threatened or did not see benefits to their constituencies; industrialists, fearing stronger competition from imports, argued that India's industrial independence would be threatened, and that they could meet India's needs from their own production. Some intellectuals attacked the reforms as being anti-socialist, antinationalist and unduly consumerist; they also argued that the benefits were restricted to the wealthier 10–15 percent of the population, and thus strengthened rather than reduced inequities in the society. Such objections in turn played into the hands of political and bureaucratic figures who saw themselves as threatened by the reforms. Immediately the elimination or sharp reduction of the regulations would cut the connection between private business and the governing party (or other parties at the state level), since there would be much less need for the payments made by businessmen for the benefits they received through the regulatory system; such a reduction would also reduce the gray incomes of the controllers. With respect to the public sector, a separation dividing the political and bureaucratic structure that oversees the operations and investments of public-sector firms, and the management of those enterprises would weaken the influence of political and bureaucratic figures over those enterprises. This would reduce their ability to use their control over output and investment decisions, say on location matters, for political purposes.

Thus, while the reforms had significant positive effects on national and industrial output, in satisfying public demands for more and better consumer goods, and in raising the degree of industrial competition, they were considered by many as partial in their effects and even inequitable. The reforms too were associated in the public mind with the continued rising price level, the effects of which harmed large segments of the population, and with a corruption that continued to pervade the system, even though formerly scarce goods were now abundant, in part as a result of the reforms.

Rajiv Gandhi never addressed the need for political changes that might bring to the surface the public dissatisfactions in the economic area. The wider spread of television reception made issues of poverty and income inequity more open than in the past. Gandhi seemed to ignore or deliberately shelve charges of corruption that struck very close to him personally, but again the free press discussed these openly and they could not be buried. The personal control that the prime minister exercised over the Congress party, which was a continuation of the practices of his mother, meant that such public dissatisfaction could not be expressed through the party. Those who disagreed with the prime minister were either relegated to powerless positions or forced to leave the party at both national and local levels. Neither the prime minister nor the Congress party faced up to those issues.

At the same time, with such central control, the power of state and local groups was severely constrained. This in part reflected the fact that in many states the Congress party no longer governed, and the national government was unwilling to take actions that might support local opposition parties. There was also no effective delegation of economic decision making and resources to the local level so that village communities could make their own decisions on felt problems. By the time the central government did make a proposal toward such delegation it was so late in the term of Rajiv Gandhi's government and regarded so much as a preelection political move that it was withdrawn before passage. Thus local energies were not effectively harnessed for economic development within regional and local geographic locations.[3] This is one reason that India has not had the surge of rural industrialization that China had. While this avoids the conflict between central macrocontrol and local investment that China has, it is at the cost of a lower level of rural industrialization and nonagricultural employment. India already has an effective macroeconomic control system. It should be possible for its policymakers to devise and introduce a system that would delegate increased economic powers and revenues to the localities to gain the benefits of local involvement in decision making and to stimulate local industrialization, but at the same time avoid the loss of macroeconomic control and the sharp booms and slumps of Chinese experience.

The economic reforms achieved positive results, but they did not go far enough in creating a sense of broader change, in terms of greater equity or reduced corruption. Those limitations contributed to the defeat of the Congress party in the 1989 national elections and the 1990 state elections.[4] There was "thunder in the air," but it had been ignored. A question after the elections was whether the new V. P. Singh government, seeking to achieve its own popular mandate, would be willing to grasp the nettle of economic reform in a major effort rather than as a series of marginal changes. Would it present an ambitious reform program that on the one hand directly addressed

the political problems of untangling the close and corrupt ties between the economic and political systems and on the other hand related the economic reforms to the perceived greater well-being of the
entire Indian population rather than of a higher-income minority?
Unfortunately it did not do that, in part because of the press of political issues upon a minority government that was dependent for its
existence on other parties with a wide range of economic perspectives, and was itself riven by factional conflicts among its leaders.
While it presented an industrial reform program going farther along
the line of liberalization, it never implemented the program. It did
present a "populist" proposal to increase the job reservations for
backward castes in government employment. This led to widespread
rioting and contributed to the government's fall in November 1990.

Its successor, an even more minority government, headed by
Chandra Shekhar, was dependent on Congress party support; while
that government adopted a tough fiscal policy, it did not have time to
present an industrial policy before it fell in early March 1991. New
elections occurred in May and June, 1991. They were the most violent
in Indian history, culminating in the murder of Rajiv Gandhi. The
Congress party won the largest number of seats, but not a majority,
and is governing with support of other secular parties. Economic
problems are more serious and there is strong need to present an effective response to them. The implementation of an economic reform
program that leads to the improvement in living conditions of the
larger portion of the Indian people would strengthen the party which
gets the credit for it, and would contribute to the continued success of
India's political democracy. Failure to do this by the hopefully more
stable coalition of parties governing after June 1991 could, on the
other hand, jeopardize Indian democracy and political stability and
even unity, as the people look for alternatives to the present democracy. These alternatives might lead to communal and religious conflicts, if they include further demands for preferences in employment
by caste or community or for separate ethnic states. In fact the new
government, faced with an economic emergency, did present a broad
reform program. Its success may be crucial for India's political future.

SOME CONTRASTS AND SIMILARITIES

What is obvious through the previous three chapters and the earlier
section of this chapter is the governing role of political needs and restraints in both initiating the reform process in the two countries,
and in controlling its development over the decade. In China the experience of the Cultural Revolution created the readiness for economic

modernization and growth as urgent policy priorities, and the victims of that decade among the party leaders became the leaders of the reform decade. The decision to initiate the reforms in the agricultural sector reflected the relative malleability of policy in that sector, which had seen frequent and drastic policy changes in the past, as well as the demands of the rural population for the type of changes that were introduced. The success in that sector created the conditions for changes in the urban sector, but the process there was politically far more sensitive, leading to a period of readjustment and balance before urban industrial reform was highlighted as policy in 1984. The sequence of industrial reform too was guided by the political sensitivities of various industrial sectors, with government planning and control remaining dominant in the heavy-industry areas considered major by the leadership, while delegation of power to enterprises and localities proceeded most rapidly in consumer goods production, agricultural processing, and foreign trade. Prices were only partially decontrolled, and that partiality contributed to corruption and black-marketing. But in the absence of an effective macrocontrol mechanism, the delegation of power and revenues to localities and enterprises combined with a politically controlled banking system, led to massive increases in credit and money supply, and to dangerous rates of inflation. The corruption and inflation, together with felt inequities and demands for greater political participation, led to political unrest, to a pulling back from reforms, and to the Tiananmen Square crackdown as the way adopted by the party leaders to deal with the political pressures.

In India too the reform process was governed by political necessities. While there was no equivalent to the Cultural Revolution as a spur to reform, Indira Gandhi began low-keyed efforts to raise industrial growth rates and improve technology by modifying the regulatory system. This shift sought to attract greater business support and to meet the demands of some sectors of the Indian population for greater availability of consumer durable goods. But these reforms were muted to avoid political difficulties. When Rajiv Gandhi came to power in 1985 after his mother's assassination, he accelerated and actively pushed wider reforms to indicate the arrival of a new, technically alert generation, to take advantage of his massive election victory, and to meet internal political demands for greater well-being. But those reforms, while well publicized, remained within the existing framework of the control system. This reflected the socialist ideology of the Congress party, but also the political realities of the Indian system, in which party funding is closely tied to business contributions induced by the regulations, and public-sector investment decisions have significant political impact. Rajiv Gandhi, unlike the Chinese leaders, did not have the option of a massive land reform, since the Indian peasants who had benefited from the first reform did not favor a second one, and land reform is a power of the states in which those peasants have great strength.

At the national level large investment in the agricultural sector to raise output has a low priority among competing claims, and would yield returns over the long run rather than in the near future. In the face of such limitations, the industrial reforms in India depended upon the demands of the top quintile of the population for greater output, while there were strong political constraints on reducing industrial controls too sharply. Those constraints also restricted the leadership from presenting an overall justification of the reforms, or a rationalization of the overall benefits. Over time too the inflationary pressures arising from continued deficit financing, and the apparently greater corruption, led first to the downplaying of the reform initiatives, and then contributed to Rajiv Gandhi's 1989 election defeat. This occurred despite significant positive economic results from the reforms, which were overshadowed by negative economic factors toward the end of Gandhi's term, as well as noneconomic issues.

In both countries, although the reforms had significant beneficial effects, the limitations on the reforms exerted by its political system and/or institutional elements in its economic system, led to their foundering. In China the Communist party's dictatorship resulted in a blockage of exchange between the party leadership and the large section of the population that was hurt by the economic developments after 1987, and which also saw various groups in strategic control positions gaining, possibly by unethical actions. During that same period in India the political limits to an accelerated or broader reform program, which might threaten business-government connections, or which might lead to strong ideological or interest-motivated opposition, resulted in a slowdown of the reform momentum and a reluctance to present an overall rationale for the specific regulatory reforms. Thus the political structures and needs of both countries, as interpreted by their governing party leaders, set the limits to reform. In China, under a dictatorship, change apparently waits for new party leaders; in India the democratic process opens up opportunities for continued reform, via future electoral competition for popular support and power and the resulting new governments.

CHAPTER SIX

A Brief Summary and Some Broader Generalizations on Reform Processes

Undertake difficult tasks by approaching what is easy in them; do great deeds by focusing on their minute aspects.

LAO TZU, *Tao Te Ching*

If you are trying to cross a chasm you don't do it in two hops.

A Polish economist, 1990

. . . [The] most dangerous moment for a bad government is generally that in which it sets about reform. Only great genius can save a prince who undertakes to relieve his subjects after a long oppression.

ALEXIS DE TOCQUEVILLE, *L'Ancien Régime*

W HAT, in summary, are the similarities and differences in the reform processes in China and India? First the characteristics that contribute to the similarities of the two economies: their great sizes; their strong agricultural character, especially with respect to employment, even as the industrial and service sectors have become more important in income terms; their low per capita incomes; and following independence and victory, the economic and political pressures and promises to raise incomes, maintain economic as well as political independence, and achieve recognition as major world powers. The longer-range goals of development in both countries have been similar since 1980, as has been a recognition of the need for changes in pre-1980 policies and institutions to achieve these goals.

In both countries the major direction of the industrial reforms was to increase the autonomy of the enterprise managers and the businessmen (in India) who ran the industrial enterprises, while simultaneously raising the incentives for desired managerial behavior to achieve the hoped-for results. Because of the size or ethnic mix of particular regions, issues of regional development and equity have been and are of major political importance in both countries. These have led to the establishment and support of enterprises that are considered socially or politically important even if economically inefficient; and thus economic criteria alone are limited in measuring their viability. Similarly in both countries, because of their size and rapidly growing labor forces, issues of employment are of major political importance and make it very difficult to shut down financially weak firms. These difficulties are strengthened by the absence of widespread social insurance or labor retraining schemes. The larger enterprises have in fact been given various social functions, performed by the state in other countries, which also limit their concentration on economic returns. In both countries too, as socialist, peasant societies, employers are assumed to have broader responsibilities for their workers in maintaining employment and providing equitable wage payments; rural patron-client systems assume certain mutual responsibilities and exchanges between patrons and dependents, even though the environment may no longer be rural.

A final, very contemporary similarity in both countries is the influence of radio and television as a stimulus for change. Radio and television sets are high-priority consumer durable goods in both countries, and the industrial reforms led to the production of far more of those goods to meet that demand. The meeting of that demand in turn had wide-ranging political effects. In both countries the watchers of television could see with their own eyes the quality of life of the wealthier groups in their society, and they wanted a taste of the same. In India this contributed to a political demand for a better life, to "thunder in the air" and to the 1989 defeat of Rajiv Gandhi. In China this stimulated a demand for more consumption goods and a greater awareness of consumption differences between social and regional groups. But it also contributed to an awareness among students and intellectuals of the changing political scene in the East European countries, and of what students and other groups were doing in those countries and such neighboring countries as South Korea to accelerate political changes. (The Chinese government as part of the reforms allowed reception of foreign broadcasts). This knowledge in turn encouraged Chinese students and intellectuals to demonstrate peacefully and protest, first in 1987 and then in 1989, to redress their grievances and ask for greater freedom. And the two sequels to the elections and protests point up again the political difference between India and China. Indian television and radio were not tightly controlled after the defeat of the government after the 1989 elections. But after Tiananmen Square, Chinese radio and television were again

placed under very tight control to prevent reception of foreign broadcasts and knowledge of foreign experience in the political area.

I will not repeat my remarks on the political constraints to the
reform process in the two countries. But the fact that China is a dictatorship and India a democracy has not only influenced the past, but
raises different potentialities for future economic reform in both
countries. In China the reform process accelerated economic growth
significantly, but the partial character of reforms, in both what they
have and have not achieved, has led to other economic problems. The
most important of these problems are the cycles of inflation followed
by forced retrenchment, and the increase in corruption resulting
from the dual price and control systems. These sharp and unsettling
economic cycles have led, among urban groups, to demands for
greater discussion of policy problems in the economic field, and for
the loosening of the party's political control. The absence of a political outlet to express public dissatisfactions has resulted in bursts of
unrest that have led, since 1989, to the reimposition of tight central
party controls over the economy and polity. On the economic side an
urgently required reform is the development of an effective macroeconomic control system to reduce those sharp economic swings.
Without this an effective microprice reform becomes politically impossible. But I am doubtful of the ability of the Communist party's
present leadership, because of its lack of economic competence in the
macroarea, or of its willingness, to take the required economic steps
to reduce both the influence of local party leaders and the possibilities of hidden sources of income. I am even more doubtful of its
willingness to widen public participation in the policy-making process. Without those changes, future economic reform and achievement will probably move along in a series of spurts and halts, but with
the spurts less strong and the halts more lengthy, as popular interest
and belief in the reform process weakens. I would be foolish to attempt to predict whether this would change, and in what manner,
once a new generation of party leaders comes into power.

In India too the reform process has been partial in character, and
not presented to the wider Indian public within a broader framework.
These limitations on the process reduced the positive economic
effects of the reforms, which were significant, but which were not felt
to have benefited large sections of the rural population or to have
dealt with issues of equity and corruption. These perceptions contributed to diminishing public support for economic reform, and
eventually to Rajiv Gandhi's defeat. But the pressures of democracy
may lead to the presentation of a more thorough and well-argued reform program not only with respect to the urban industrial sector, but

also in the agricultural sector, by a governing party or group of parties seeking continued popular support after the 1991 national elections. If such a broad program is articulated and implemented it could lead to more rapid industrial and economic growth, with a wider spread of benefits to the Indian public than in the past. If however this is not done, and the economy returns to the relatively low Hindu rate of growth, or if the beneficiaries of a somewhat faster growth are considered to be a privileged group, this might well prove harmful for Indian democracy. Then an expectant but disappointed public might well explore nondemocratic alternatives for answers to the economic policy questions, or seek improvement by such measures as ethnic or religious preferences.

This then is my final contrast of the reform processes in the two countries. The demands for continued economic reform in China might undermine the existing political system that combines a Communist party dictatorship with a significant delegation of economic power, related to political power, to local and provincial party leaders and government agencies. That political threat may narrowly limit the extent to which Communist party leaders are willing to expand economic reform in the future. In India however, the demands for continued economic reform could strengthen the democratic political system as various parties compete for public political support by presenting broader and stronger economic reform programs. But failure to accelerate the process and expand the benefits of economic reform in India might undermine its democracy by weakening the support of the wider public, if it comes to feel that it has not received the benefits expected from over forty years of democratic socialism.

What light do the Chinese and Indian experiences with economic reform throw on the economic reform efforts in other countries, not only the former Soviet Bloc countries in Eastern Europe and elsewhere, but also democracies, including the United States? It is very clear that economic reform is a political process, like any more limited change in economic policy. This means that the possible outer limits of a reform process will be determined by political support for the process, of which an important element is the ability of the political leadership of a country to build upon, or develop, popular demands or support for economic change. Similarly the restraints upon the reform process are set by the lack of popular support for economic change. But economic reform is not simply a broad, overall process; it may point in a general direction, but the changes in policy are specific. To develop those specific components of a broader reform program requires both the support of particular groups in the public who see themselves benefiting from the changes, and the neutralization of the opposition of groups that might feel themselves harmed. The latter groups might be members of the bureaucracy, or of a political party who would lose power from the changes, or of economic interest groups that would lose by the change. That opposition can be neutralized by wider public support for reform, or by the possibility of benefits to the potential opposition that would compensate for the threatened losses. In addition, such changes occur within a broad ideological system, whether in the form of an economic belief, such as socialism or capitalism, or of national aspirations. If the reforms can be shown to be consistent with a country's ideological framework, that will contribute to their acceptance; if the leadership is unable to persuade the public of such consistency, acceptance will prove more difficult.

The great advantage of the economic reform process in such East European countries as Poland and Czechoslovakia is that it takes place on the wave of a political revolution that overthrew the previous Communist rule and ideology. With that revolution a reform that completely overthrows the economic system of the former political rulers also becomes possible—and this is apparently what is occurring with popular support. But the previous socialisms also had ideals of equity and full employment that may set limits to support for a free market economy. A Swedish or French model of democratic mixed socialism may be more compatible with the past ideals than full-fledged capitalism, and such a goal may have greater public appeal in the reforming countries than a United States or Conservative English model.

In East European countries in which economic reform is felt to be necessary but political revolutions of a magnitude comparable to those in Poland and Czechoslovakia have not occurred, the Chinese reform model may be more likely, characterized by a tension, which can become threatening to the ruling party leaders, between the process and results of economic reforms and their continued rule. Some of those leaders however may see the necessity of a continued dialogue with the wider public on the economic reforms, in the light of the experiences of neighboring countries in which party rule has been overthrown and in view of the threat to their own party rule. The Chinese experience too makes clear that macroeconomic reform must accompany microreform in previously soviet-type economies, which do not have macrocontrol systems, in order to reduce the risks of inflation. Also the development of an adequate social-security system, encompassing worker retraining, will reduce the pressures to support uneconomic industrial enterprises for the sake of maintaining jobs.

The Indian reform experience provides an example of the democratic reform process. Here the debate over reform is a public process occurring through the press, the radio and television system, and then in the legislature, rather than one confined to party leaders. Public support is necessary, based on a conviction that the reforms are necessary to deal with a critical situation. In India the major reforms in the agricultural sector that led to the Green Revolution were induced by the crop failures and threat of famine in the 1960s. There was no such overhanging emergency in the industrial sector in the 1980s, but rather a sense of lack of progress and of failed expectations, and that some policy changes were necessary to meet these issues. The reforms were therefore moderate, within the framework of the existing regulatory system and consistent with India's version of its socialism and nationalism. They accomplished the goals of raising industrial output, increasing competition, and expanding foreign trade, but they were limited in their results.

India's experience with economic reforms might thus be comparable to that of the United States. In both countries there has been an ability to respond to a crisis—in the United States the Depression of the 1930s ushered in the New Deal and the welfare state.[1] Those major reforms were introduced within the framework of a capitalist ideology, comparable in style to India carrying out its earlier agricultural policy reforms within a socialist ideological framework. I remarked earlier on some similarities of current macroproblems—government deficit, slow inflation, balance-of-payments difficulties—in the two countries, and in the difficulties the two governments face in dealing with them. Both of these examples and their similarities may reflect the continuous character of economic policies in a democracy as opposed to a dictatorship, with changes in policy normally of an incremental nature, except in an emergency, when public support can be aroused for massive reform. Extensive reform in noncrisis conditions calls for a long-term political leadership committed to the need for reform and prepared to exercise a strong initiative. Without this it may not be possible to maintain momentum in the face of competing claims not only upon the leaders, but upon the attention and interest of the wider voting public.

NOTES

1. L. Rudolph and S. Rudolph, *In Pursuit of Lakshmi* (Chicago, 1988), p. 336, table 40. (These figures are as of 1971–72.) The term "bullock capitalist" was first used in this book.

2. S. Swamy, *Economic Growth in China and India* (New Delhi, 1989).

CHAPTER ONE

1. Tang Tsou, *The Cultural Revolution and Post-Mao Reforms* (Chicago, 1986), pp. 116–17.

2. Ibid., p. 71.

3. Ibid., pp. 130–32.

4. Ibid., p. 176; see also pp. 178–79 on this issue.

5. Ibid., p. 94; also Lynn White III, *Policies of Chaos* (Princeton, 1989) on the Cultural Revolution.

6. E. Vogel, *One Step Ahead in China* (Cambridge, MA, 1989), p. 42. Vogel quotes the remarks of a leader of Guangdong province.

7. Quotations are from Deng Xiaopong, *Fundamental Issues in Present-Day China* (Oxford, 1987), pp. 67 (1984); 122–24 (Aug. 1985); 130–32 (Sept. 1985); 140 (Jan. 1986).

8. Ibid., pp. 153–55 (Sept. 1986).

9. Ibid., pp. 162–65 (Dec. 30, 1986); and 169–70 (Jan. 13, 1987).

10. Ibid., p. 192 (June 1987).

11. Ibid., p. 31 (1983); on political reform see also pp. 150–53 (Sept. 1986).

12. D. J. Solinger, *China's Business under Socialism* (Berkeley, 1987), pp. 298–99. The entire book argues the theme of this summary quotation.

13. D. S. G. Goodman, "Political Perspectives," in *China's Regional Development*, ed. D. S. G. Goodman (London, 1989), pp. 20–37; quotation pp. 22–23; also pp. 30–31. See ibid., introduction by Kirkby and Cannon, pp. 7–12, on regional policies and the "security" dispersion.

14. See Barry Naughton, "The Third Front: Defence Industrialization in the Chinese Interior," *China Quarterly*, no. 115 (Sept. 1988): 351–86. Naughton estimates that over half of the industrial investment in China in

this period was in the interior provinces, under the "Third Front" defense program. P. 366.

15. For a good review of the shifts in central control over industry, see C. Wong, "Material Allocation and Decentralization," pp. 257–62 in E. Perry and C. Wong, *The Political Economy of Reform in Post-Mao China* (Cambridge, MA, 1985).

16. Athar Hussain, "Enterprise Reform in China" (Paper presented in Beijing, April 1989), p. 11.

17. V. Shue, *The Reach of the State* (Stanford, 1988), pp. 134–35. See also chap. 4.

18. Ibid., pp. 143–44 (her emphasis).

19. W. Byrd and Lin Quigsong, *China's Rural Industry* (Washington, DC, 1990), p. 10.; see too the paper by Jean C. Oi, "Economic Management and Rural Government," presented at the 1990 meeting of the Association for Asian Studies, p. 6 (table 1). D. Granick's *Chinese State Enterprises: A Regional Property Rights Analysis* (Chicago, 1990) is still another very recent examination of the functioning of China's industries at the regional level, but looks at the state-owned sector. Granick also centers upon the power of regional authorities in this sector, a power based upon local property rights with respect to those enterprises.

20. On some of these issues as they apply to China, I found the following references illuminating: R. Taylor, "Chinese Hierarchy in Comparative Perspective," *Journal of Asian Studies*, vol. 48, no. 3 (Aug. 1989): 490–511; M. M. Yang, "The Gift Economy and State Power in China," *Comparative Studies in Society and History*, vol. 31, no. 1 (Jan. 1989): 25–54; P. A. Cohen, "The Post-Mao Reforms in Historical Perspective," *Journal of Asian Studies*, vol. 47, no. 3 (Aug. 1988): 519–41; and A. Walder, *Communist Neo-Traditionalism* (Berkeley, 1986). See on the more general issue of a peasant society: J. Scott, *Moral Economy of a Peasant Society* (New Haven, 1976); and my own *Peasant Society in a Changing Economy* (Urbana, 1975). On Chinese nationalism see J. Townsend, "Nationalism Chinese Style," *Antioch Review*, vol. 46, no. 2 (Spring 1988): 204–20.

21. See P. N. Dhar, "India since Independence," *Times of India* (Bombay), Dec. 12–16, 1988; quotation Dec. 12, 1988, p. 12. Dhar, one of India's leading economists, also played a significant policy-making role in the 1970s.

22. Raj Krishna, "Ideology and Economic Policy," *Indian Economic Review*, vol. 23, no. 1 (Jan.–June 1988): 1–26, quotations on pp. 3, 4, 5–6. This article was written in 1984 but was posthumously published. Raj Krishna had been economics professor at Delhi University and a member of the planning commission during the Janata party government.

23. P. N. Dhar, "India since Independence," Dec. 12, 1988, p. 12.

24. P. N. Dhar, "The Political Economy of Development in India," *Indian Economic Review*, vol. 22, no. 1 (Jan.–June 1987): 13–15.

25. P. N. Dhar, "India since Independence," Dec. 13, 1988, p. 14. We shall examine the economic situation at the start of the reform program in detail in the next chapter.

26. On the general issue of India's political economy, see among other recent writing: P. K. Bardhan, *The Political Economy of Development in India* (Oxford, 1984); Rudolph and Rudolph, *In Pursuit of Lakshmi*; Dhar, "The Political Economy of Development in India"; S. A. Kochanek, "Briefcase Politics in India: The Congress Party and the Business Elite," *Asian Survey*,

vol. 27, no. 12 (Dec. 1987): 1278–1301; and A. Vaidyanathan, "State and Economic Development in India," *Bulletin of the Madras Institute of Development Studies*, vol. 19, no. 1, (Jan. 1989): 48–60. On the size of the underground economy, see D. R. Pendse, *Black Money and Budgets* (New Delhi, 1984), pp. 37–38.

27. Subsidy data from P. K. Bardhan, *Political Economy*, pp. 61–63; income data from C. T. Kurien, "Indian Economy in the 1980s and on to the 1990s," *Bulletin of the Madras Institute of Development Studies*, vol. 19, no. 1 (Jan. 1989): 38–41; price data from Rudolph and Rudolph, *In Pursuit of Lakshmi*, p. 237, table 27.

28. Dhar, "India since Independence," Dec. 13, 1988, p. 14.

29. On the IRDP, see R. Pulley's *Making the Poor Creditworthy* (Washington, DC, 1989); and S. Ranade, "The Political Economy of Poverty Allocation in Rural India" (typewritten draft, 1989), chaps. 1 and 2.

30. One of the most comprehensive reviews of the poverty issue in India is by J. K. Mukhopadhyay, "Estimates of Poverty Statistics in India: A Close Look," *Journal of Income and Wealth* (Bombay), vol. 10, no. 1 (Jan. 1988): 67–76. See also, in R. E. B. Lucas and G. F. Papanek, eds., *The Indian Economy* (Boulder, 1988), the papers by A. M. Khusro, G. F. Papanek, and A. Vaidyanathan. Ranade, "Political Economy," on p. 13 gives a table showing a decline in the poverty ratio in rural India from 57 percent in 1960–61 to 40 percent in 1984–85; the number below the line rose from 200 million to 220 million.

31. On the peasant society, see note 20, above; my own book referred to in that note discusses India.

32. The degree of "urban bias" in favor of city dwellers is probably less in India than in China, in part because India's rural inhabitants can move to the cities and in part because India's democracy gives the large rural population significant power, especially at the state level where much of agricultural policy is made. On the extent of China's urban bias see D. G. Johnson, *The People's Republic of China, 1978–1990* (San Francisco, 1991).

CHAPTER TWO

1. There is a very large literature on China's pre-1980 economic experience which I quickly summarize here in the text. It is so large that I will not give specific references except when I use direct quotations. I might simply add that John K. Fairbank's *The Great Chinese Revolution, 1800–1985* (New York, 1986) puts the communist revolution and rule within the broader context of Chinese history, to which it is an excellent and unique introduction for the nonexpert. I also refer to Jonathan D. Spence's more recent book, *The Search for Modern China* (New York, 1990) for a similar effort, but over a longer period of time, from about 1600 to 1989.

2. C. P. Wong, "Between Plan and Market: The Role of the Local Sector in Post-Mao China," *Journal of Comparative Economics*, vol. 11 (1987): 387–89. This and two other articles by Wong are the best introduction I know to the complex and very confusing system of enterprises and controls in Communist China: "Material Allocation and Decentralization," in Perry and Wong, *Political Economy*, esp. pp. 257–68; and "Ownership and Control in Chinese Industry . . . ," in U.S. Congress, Joint Economic Committee,

China's Economy Looks toward the Year 2000 (Washington, DC, 1986), pp. 571–603.

3. See pp. 111 and 118–25 in J. Prybla, *The Chinese Economy*, 2d ed. (Columbia, SC, 1981) on the planning mechanism.

4. On this network of controls over the Shenyang Smelter, see W. A. Byrd, *The Shenyang Smelter* (World Bank Staff Working Paper 766; Washington, DC, 1985), pp. 32–35.

5. O. Laaksonen, *Management in China during and after Mao in Enterprises, Government, and Party* (New York, 1988), pp. 202–3, 283, and 286.

6. H. Harding, *China's Second Revolution: Reform after Mao* (Washington, DC, 1987), p. 15.

7. B. Naughton, "The Third Front," p. 381.

8. *Beijing Review*, vol. 31, no. 26 (June 27, 1988): 11.

9. Ma Hong, *New Strategy for China's Economy* (Beijing, 1983). Quotations are from pp. 14–15, 18–19, 20, 23, 25, and 26. I have also paraphrased extensively.

10. Complementing Ma Hong's remarks on wages, Andrew Walder in a review of wage reforms in China notes that wages were "virtually" frozen from 1963 to 1977, with workers entering the labor market after 1963 struck at the lowest levels of pay; bonuses were also abolished in 1967. "There simply was no relationship between work performance and pay." A. G. Walder, "Wage Reform and the Web of Factory Interests," *China Quarterly*, no. 109 (March 1987): 23–24.

11. *Beijing Review*, vol. 27, no. 44, supplement (Oct. 29, 1984), "Decision of the Central Committee of the Communist Party of China on Reform of the Economic Structure" (Adopted Oct. 20, 1984), pp. iv, v.

12. The manufacturing sector as defined in India includes a large number of small-scale enterprises, many of which are not classified as factories.

13. N. Desai, "Development Planning in Review" (Paper prepared for ICSSR seminar "India since Independence," Dec. 26–30, 1988), pp. 7–8; see also I. J. Ahluwalia, *Industrial Growth in India* (Delhi, 1985), chap. 2.

14. V. K. R. V. Rao, *India's National Income: 1950–1980* (New Delhi, 1983), p. 61; and my book *Industrial Change in India, 1970–2000* (Riverdale, MD, 1988); see esp. chaps. 1–3 for the material in this chapter.

15. R. Thomas, *India's Emergence as an Industrial Power* (New Delhi, 1982), p. 3.

16. GOI, *Report of the Committee to Examine Principles of Shift from Physical to Financial Controls* (The Narasimhan Committee Report), (1985), p. 1. See too I. J. Ahluwalia, *Industrial Growth in India*, which is indispensable on its subject.

17. That is C. T. Kurien's expression in his "Indian Economy in the 1980s and on to the 1990s," p. 41.

18. K. S. Krishnaswamy, "What Ails the Public Sector?" (Fourth Agit Bhagat Memorial Lecture, Ahmedabad, India, 1980).

19. L. K. Jha, *Mr. Red Tape* (New Delhi, 1987), pp. 180–81; p. 203 for quotations, but see chaps. 13 and 14 in general.

20. Ibid and Krishnaswamy, "What Ails the Public Sector?."

21. Desai, "Development Planning in Review," p. 9; quotation from Rao, *India's National Income*, p. 15.

22. Dhar, "The Political Economy of Development in India," pp. 5–6. One of the best recent analyses of the effects of India's industrial control sys-

tem upon technology development in India is A. V. Desai, ed., *Technology Absorption in Indian Industry* (New Delhi, 1988). On small-scale industries a very good overview for the pre-1980 period is J. C. Sandesara, *Small Industry in India* (Ahmedabad, 1980).

23. On this see J. Riedel et al., "Determinants of Indian Export Performance in the 1970s," *Weltwirtschaftliches Archiv*, vol. 120, no. 1, (1984): 56.

24. GOI, *Economic Survey, 1984–85* (New Delhi, 1985), pp. 33–34.

25. I. G. Patel, "On Taking India into the Twenty First Century: New Economic Policy in India," *Modern Asian Studies*, vol. 21, no. 2 (1987): 216.

26. C. T. Kurien, "Planning and Institutional Transformation of the Indian Economy," *Social Scientist*, vol. 15, no. 7 (1987): 26.

27. V. K. R. V. Rao, "India since Independence," *Mainstream*, Jan. 28, 1989, p. 18 (his emphasis). See also on these issues the recent stimulating and insightful book by V. S. Naipaul, *India: A Million Mutinies Now* (New York, 1990).

28. There had been earlier efforts at liberalization, beginning with Indira Gandhi's devaluation of the rupee in 1966.

CHAPTER THREE

1. C. C. Lin, "The Reinstatement of Economics in China Today," *China Quarterly* (March 1981): 1–48, quotation pp. 43–44.

2. Ibid.

3. See Harding, *China's Second Revolution*, pp. 55–57; C. C. Lin, "Reinstatement of Economics," pp. 43–44; PRC, State Statistical Bureau, *Statistical Yearbook of China, 1986* (Hong Kong, 1986), pp. 535–36 on prices and p. 481 on foreign trade.

4. Y. W. Sung and T. M. H. Chan, "China's Economic Reforms I: The Debates in China," *Asian-Pacific Economic Literature*, vol. 1, no. 1 (May 1987): 1–25, quotation on p. 4. See also Lin, "Reinstatement of Economics," pp. 34–37.

5. Lin, "Reinstatement of Economics"; Sung and Chan, "China's Economic Reforms."

6. On the agricultural reforms see Sung and Chan, "China's Economic Reforms," p. 2; Perry and Wong, *Political Economy*, pp. 10–11; and World Bank, *China: Finance and Investment* (Washington, DC, 1988), p. 6.

7. Oi, "Economic Management," p. 6. Her paper also presents a more detailed picture of the tax reforms themselves, and of the complex variety of local taxes on industry which in effect replaced the highly centralized fiscal system under Mao.

8. P. Nolan and Dong Fureng, eds., *Market Forces in China* (London, 1990), esp. chaps. 1 and 2 by Nolan, chap. 3 by C. Brammel, and chap. 4 by Dong Fureng.

9. *Beijing Review, China Today (3): Economic Readjustment and Reform* (Beijing, 1982), esp. pp. 27–38; quotation on pp. 30–31.

10. *Beijing Review, China Today (3)*, pp. 30–31.

11. PRC, *Statistical Yearbook of China, 1986* pp. 535, 481 and 20.

12. *Beijing Review, China Today*, pp. 9–10.

13. Lin Zhoufou, "The Price Situation," in ibid., pp. 204n. and 206–7.

14. PRC, *Statistical Yearbook of China, 1986*, p. 481.

15. See *Beijing Review,* "Decision of the Central Committee," pp. iii–viii.

16. Ibid.

17. Ibid., p. viii from the section titled "Establish a Rational Price System . . ."

18. Ibid., p. ix.

19. PRC, *Statistical Yearbook of China, 1986,* p. 535.

20. Zhao Ziyang, "Advance along the Road of Socialism with Chinese Characteristics," *Documents of the Thirteenth National Congress of the Communist Party of China* (Beijing, 1987). see esp. pt. 4, pp. xi–xv.

21. Ibid., sect. 4.

22. Ibid., sect. 5.

23. See *Beijing Review,* vol. 31, no. 21 (May 23, 1988): 10 for actual price change.

24. Ibid., no. 22 (May 30, 1988): 9; no. 24 (June 13, 1988): 9–10.

25. Li Peng, "Resolutely Carry out the Principles of Improvement, Rectification and Deepened Reform—Report on the Work of the Government" (March 20, 1989), in *Beijing Review,* vol. 32, no. 16 (April 17, 1989). Supplement centerfold, pp. ii, iii, and viii for quotations. One of the best reviews of the 1988 price reform and its collapse is L. Dittmer, "China in 1988," *Asian Survey,* vol. 29, no. 1 (Jan. 1989): 12–28, esp. 19–24.

26. Atul Kohli, "Politics of Economic Liberalization in India," *World Development,* vol. 17, no. 3, pp. 306–11.

27. On Indira Gandhi's liberalization see Ahluwalia, *Industrial Growth in India,* chap. 8; GOI, Planning Commission, *The Seventh Five Year Plan, 1985–90* (New Delhi, 1985), vol. 1, chap. 1, pp. 2–3; vol. 2, chap. 7, esp. pp. 167–69.

28. Ahluwalia, *Industrial Growth,* p. 150.

29. A. Kohli, "Politics," p. 311.

30. F. A. Mehta, "Growth, Controls and the Private Sector," in Lucas and Papanek, eds., *Indian Economy,* p. 203.

31. Centre for Monitoring the Indian Economy (CMIE), *The Liberalization Process* (Bombay, 1986), introduction, p. i. (This is the most detailed presentation of all the liberalization measures from 1985 onward that I know; interestingly, this center is a private organization, not connected to government.)

32. T. L. Sankar and Y. V. Reddy, eds., *Privatization* (Hyderabad, 1989), p. 72.

33. GOI, *The Seventh Five Year Plan,* vol. 1, chap. 2, p. 9.

34. Ibid., pp. 16 and 17.

35. Ibid., p. 45.

36. Ibid.

37. Ibid., vol. 2, pp. 170–72.

38. Ibid., pp. 175, 191–94; see D. R. Pendse, "The Message of the Seventh Five Year Plan," Inaugural Lecture, Dr. Helekar Memorial Lecture Series, Goa (Feb. 7, 1986), pp. 2–3.

39. See I. J. Ahluwalia, "Industrial Policy and Industrial Performance in India," pp. 154–55 in Lucas and Papanek, eds., *Indian Economy.* The term "broadbanding" refers to a practice that permits an enterprise to produce related products other than its narrowly defined licensed product, from any idle

capacity it might have (as allowing an automobile manufacturer to produce trucks, or vice versa, from otherwise idle equipment).

40. G. Gouri, "Economic Liberalization in India," pp. 58–60 in Sankar and Reddy, eds., *Privitization*; CMIE, *Liberalization Process*.

41. CMIE, *Liberalization Process*, pp. 91–97.

42. Ibid., p. ii.

43. On tax policies see S. Acharya, "India's Fiscal Policy," esp. pp. 300–306, in Lucas and Papanek, eds., *Indian Economy*; and CMIE, *Liberalization Process*, pp. 85–87. On capital issues policies see ibid., pp. 84–85.

44. Mehta, "Growth," pp. 204–5.

45. Ibid., pp. 203, 205.

46. Kohli, "Politics," pp. 313–16.

47. Ibid.

48. P. N. Dhar, "Indian Economy . . . ," pp. 17–18 in Lucas and Papanek, eds., *Indian Economy*.

49. Dhar, "India since Independence," esp. the Dec. 16, 1988, article, p. 12.

50. Vaidyanathan, "State and Economic Development in India," pp. 59–60.

CHAPTER FOUR

1. In what follows I have used many sources. Among these some of the most useful are: Luo Yuanzheng, "Structural Reform and Economic Development in China," *International Social Science Journal*, no. 120 (May 1989): 189–201; Chen Yizi et al., "Reform: Results and Lessons from the 1985 CESRRI Survey," *Journal of Comparative Economics*, vol. 11 (1987): 462–78; Dong Fureng, " 'Losing Shape' in Course of Reform," FBIS-CHI-88-251 (Dec. 30, 1988), pp. 31ff.; Zhang Zhongli, "The Chinese Economic Regulatory Mechanism in Transformation," *Journal of Asian Economics*, vol. 1, no. 1; and C. C. Chien, "The Recent Inflation in the People's Republic of China" (Paper presented for the Conference on U.S.-Asia Economic Relations, New York City, June 18–22, 1989). Among recent papers by non-Chinese authors, see A. Hussain, "Enterprise Reform in China," and his "Chinese Economic Reforms: Irregularities and Crimes" (Paper presented at Harvard University, May 1988); J. S. Prybyla, "China's Economic Experiment: Back from the Market?" *Problems of Communism* (Jan.–Feb. 1989): 1–18; and D. J. Solinger, "Capitalist Measures with Chinese Characteristics," ibid., 19–33. Also see Solinger's "Economic Reform in China," *Harvard International Review*, vol. 11, no. 2, pp. 16–18. I will not give further detailed references to the above items unless I quote directly; I will give detailed references to other sources.

2. Much of the data in this and the four following paragraphs are from Luo Yuanzheng, "Structural Reform," supplemented by Prybyla, "China's Economic Experiment."

3. On the two-tier price system see K. Ishimura, "China's Multiple Price System," *Japan External Trade Organization, China Newsletter*, no. 80 (May–June 1989): 2–9.

4. D. Perkins, "Reforming China's Economic System," *Journal of Economic Literature*, vol. 26, no. 2 (June 1988): 627–28.

5. Luo, "Structural Reform."

6. Ibid.

7. "More State Units Run at a Deficit," *China Daily* (Beijing), May 13, 1987, p. 3; and Solinger, "Capitalist Measures."

8. Luo, "Structural Reform."

9. Ibid.

10. Ibid.

11. Solinger, *Problems*, pp. 19–20 and 28–33; and Solinger, "Economic Reform," p. 17.

12. Hussain, "Enterprise Reform in China," pp. 12–13.

13. Ibid., pp. 13–14.

14. A Chinese friend of mine has compared the provinces to families, and as Chinese families with higher incomes want consumer durables, so provinces wish to have the capabilities to produce those goods as their revenues rise.

15. Chen Yizi et al., "Reform," pp. 474–77.

16. C. Findlay, P. Mayer, and A. Watson, "Fighting for the Fleece" (Mimeo, Sept. 1989); quotation, p. 6. See also, on VTEs, T. Manohoran, "Current Rural Organizational Structure in the PRC" (Mimeo, Jan. 1990), esp. pp. 15ff; B. Jacobs, "Political and Economic Organizational Changes . . . in Several Rural Chinese Localities," *Australian Journal of Chinese Affairs*, no. 14 (July 1985): 105–30. See also, of course, Oi, "Economic Management"; Byrd and Lin, eds., *China's Rural Industry*; and Nolan and Dong Fureng, eds., *Market Forces in China*, on the growth of rural industry.

17. Mayer et al., "Fighting over Fleece," p. 7.

18. Ibid., p. 14.

19. Jacobs, "Political and Economic Organizational Changes," p. 127.

20. Byrd and Lin, eds., *China's Rural Industry*, p. 16.

21. Nolan and Dong Fureng, eds., *Market Forces in China*, pp. 14–15.

22. See "China's Economy: A Survey," *Economist*, vol. 304, no. 7509 (Aug. 1, 1987): 10, 15, and 17; Chen Yizi et al., "Reform," pp. 474–75; Perkins, "Reforming China's Economic System," pp. 619 and 629–30.

23. Chien, "Recent Inflation," pp. 17–27.

24. PRC, State Statistical Bureau, *China Statistical Abstract, 1989*, ed. W. T. Liu (New York, 1989), tables T 7.24 and 7.25 (pp. 86–87).

25. Chien, "Recent Inflation."

26. PRC, *China Statistical Abstract, 1989*.

27. Hussain, "Chinese Economic Reforms." This is one of the best discussions of Chinese corruption and irregularities since the reforms that I have seen.

28. Ibid.

29. Chinese economic data over time are both difficult to interpret and difficult to reconcile. This reflects the weakening or breaking up of the data collection system for political purposes, the crudeness of the data, and a reliance on Marxist categories of classification which have to be translated or adjusted to place the data on a comparable basis with other countries of the world. But over the past decade qualified analysts consider that the data do meet international standards.

30. Harding, *China's Second Revolution*, p. 106 (table 5.1); Perkins, "Reforming China's Economic System," pp. 612 (table 1), 627, and 628 (table 4); G. Tidrick and C. Jiyuan, *China's Industrial Reform* (Washington, DC, 1987),

p. 2 (table 1.1). Where the data in these tables have appeared consistent from table to table, I have combined them to extend their time period, where this was useful. See too R. E. Feinberg et al., *Economic Reform in Three Giants* (New Brunswick, 1990), p. 79.

31. The data on total industrial output and type in this paragraph are from the PRC, *China Statistical Abstract, 1989*, tables T 1.10–1.12 (pp. 10–11).

32. P. Nolan, in Nolan and Fureng, *Market Forces*, p. 17.

33. On the investment levels by sector see R. F. Dernberger and R. S. Eckaus, *Financing Asian Development*, vol. 2, *China and India* (Lanham, MD, 1988), esp. Dernberger's chap. 2 on China, pp. 35–39 (including table 5 on pp. 36–37); see also PRC, *China Statistical Abstract, 1989*, tables T 1.5 (p. 6), T 1.9 (p. 9), T. 6.9–6.11 (pp. 61–62).

34. On foreign trade see among others, Harding, *China's Second Revolution*, pp. 136–49, but especially tables 6.1 (p. 139) and 6.2 (p. 140); also Perkins, "Reforming China's Economic System," pp. 621–22; PRC, *China Statistical Abstract, 1989*, table T 7.17 (p. 82).

35. J. C. Hsu, *China's Foreign Trade Reforms* (Cambridge, 1989), pp. 76–91, including tables 3.7 and 3.8 and the section "Commodity composition of China's trade with Hong Kong."

36. Harding, *China's Second Revolution*, pp. 141–44.

37. Ibid. See also C. Farnsworth's article "U.S. Shifts Complaints on Trade" in the *New York Times* (Chicago ed.), March 30, 1991, p. 15, for 1990 data on China-U.S. trade.

38. PRC, *China Statistical Abstract, 1989*, table T 7.21 (p. 84); and Harding, *China's Second Revolution*, p. 144. (Chinese data separates overseas Chinese from those from Hong Kong, Macao, and Taiwan—that is irrelevant for my analysis.)

39. Harding, "China's Second Revolution, pp. 159–63; PRC, *China Statistical Abstract, 1989*, table T 7.19 (p. 83).

40. Harding, *China's Second Revolution*, p. 171.

41. On the issue of productivity see Swamy, *Economic Growth*, pp. 126–34; Perkins, "Reforming China's Economic System," pp. 627–31 (table 4 on p. 628); Dernberger and Eckaus, *Financing Asian Development*, pp. 46–47 and table A2, pp. 65–66. For the most thorough discussion of the literature of measurement difficulties and of varying results see Chen Kuan et al., together with G. H. Jefferson and T. G. Rawski, "Productivity Change in Chinese Industry: 1953–1985," *Journal of Comparative Economics*, vol. 12 (1988): 570–91, with quotations from pp. 585–86. (I have given the Cobb-Douglas function results of these authors' research rather than the higher trans-log results, because the former are more comparable internationally.) For an international comparison see Swamy, *Economic Growth*, pp. 126–29.

42. Dittmer, *China in 1988*, p. 21.

43. Luo Yuanzheng, "Structural Reform," pp. 199–200.

44. Ibid.

45. "Li Peng on Current Economic Issues," in *Beijing Review*, vol. 33, no. 44 (Oct. 29–Nov. 4, 1990): 16–21; and "Commodity Prices Stabilized, Readjusted," in *Beijing Review*, vol. 34. no. 5 (Feb. 4–10, 1991): 19–22. See also articles by N. D. Kristof and S. WuDunn in the *New York Times* of Feb. 19, 1990; March 5, 1990; Aug. 26, 1990; and March 26, 1991. A quite favorable interpretation of China's recent economic policy moves by N. Lardy,

"Sustaining Development" (mimeo) is summarized in the *Woodrow Wilson Center Report*, vol. 2, no. 5 (March 1991): 1–2.

46. Dong Fureng, " 'Losing Shape,' " p. 50.

47. Three recent studies which I have found very useful for the India section of this chapter are J. Echeverri-Gent, "Economic Reform in India . . . ," chap. 3 in Feinberg et al., *Economic Reform in Three Giants*; T. N. Ninan, "Business and Economy . . . ," chap. 2 in M. Bouton and P. Oldenburg, eds., *India Briefing, 1989* (Boulder, CO, 1989); and J. Adams, "Breaking Away . . . ," chap. 4 in M. Bouton and P. Oldenburg, eds., *India Briefing, 1990* (Boulder, CO, 1990).

48. Very much of this discussion of the electronics industry is based on K. J. Joseph, "Growth Performance of Indian Electronics under Liberalization," *Economic and Political Weekly* (Bombay), vol. 24 (Aug. 19, 1989): 1915–20.

49. On the small-scale sector see ILO-ARTEP, *Employment and Structural Change in Indian Industries* (Geneva, 1989), pp. 27–29.

50. On producers in other fields see *India Today*, "Getting into Stride" (Jan. 15, 1990, Special Issue), p. 35.

51. CMIE, *Production*, pp. S37–38, on the cement industry, and pp. 7 (table 1.4) and S35–36 on other housing products. On cement, M. S. Adiseshiah, *Mid-Year Review of the Indian Economy: 1987–88* (New Delhi, 1988), p. 125; and I. J. Ahluwalia, "Comments on Prof. J. C. Sandesara's paper" (Paper given at the ICSSR Seminar, Dec. 26–30, 1988, mimeo), p. 7.

52. F. A. Mehta, "Growth," pp. 209–10.

53. Ibid.

54. Echeverri-Gent, "Economic Reform," pp. 110–11; Ninan, "Business and Economy," pp. 44–45.

55. GOI, Tata Services, *Statistical Outline of India, 1989–90*, Glossary, p. 224.

56. GOI, Ministry of Finance, *Economic Survey, 1988–89* (New Delhi, 1989), pp. 53–56; Tata Services, *Statistical Outline of India, 1989–90*, pp. 82 (table 80) and 130 (tables 136, 137); Ninan, "Business and Economy," p. 47; World Bank, *India: An Industrializing Economy in Transition* (Washington, DC, 1989), p. 31.

57. On the central government sector see J. C. Sandesara, "Public Sector in India," (University of Baroda, D. K. Shukla Memorial Lecture, Feb. 23, 1991; mimeo), pp. 15–16; also Echeverri-Gent, "Economic Reform," pp. 121–22. On state government enterprises, see T. L. Sankar et al., "State Level Public Enterprises in India," *Economic and Political Weekly*, vol. 24, no. 8 (Feb. 25, 1989): M33–40; and Tata Services, *Statistical Outline, 1989–90*, p. 81 (table 79).

58. Sankar et al., "State Level Public Enterprises," p. M40.

59. Ninan, "Business and Economy," pp. 37–39; and Adams, "Breaking Away," p. 87; Ahluwalia, "Comments," pp. 5–6; Tata Services, *Statistical Outline, 1989–90*, pp. 69 (table 68) and 89 (table 89).

60. Annual import figures from J. Echeverri-Gent, "Economic Reform," p. 120.

61. Composition of imports, GOI *Economic Survey, 1988–89* pp. S-72 and S-73; *Economic Survey, 1987–88*, p. 36.

62. Author's interviews in India in 1988.

63. K. J. Joseph, "Growth Performance," p. 1919.

64. GOI, *Economic Survey, 1988–89*, pp. S-72 to S-75.

65. Data on exports from GOI, *Economic Survey, 1988–89*, pp. S-74–75 and 109–14; J. Echeverri-Gent, "Economic Reform," p. 120; Tata Services, *Statistical Outline, 1988–89*, p. 96 (table 97); and World Bank, *India*, p. 240 (table 3.2).

66. For interpretation see two chapters in Lucas and Papanek, eds., *Indian Economy:* chap. 11, D. Nayyar, "India's Export Performance, 1970–85," esp. pp. 230–32; and chap. 13, C. D. Wadhva, "Some Aspects of India's Export Policy and Performance," esp. pp. 276–78. For estimates of profitability in domestic markets in India and export markets, see World Bank, *India*, pp. 157–58 (including table 4.10).

67. Nayyar, "India's Export Performance," p. 230.

68. Wadhva, "Some Aspects of India's Export Policy," p. 277.

69. Ibid.

70. Echeverri-Gent, "Growth Performance," pp. 119–20; Ninan, "Business and Economy," pp. 36 and 56.

71. Echeverri-Gent, "Growth Performance," pp. 113–15; Ninan, "Business and Economy," pp. 51–52 (p. 52 for quotation); C. Rangarajan, "India's Foreign Borrowing," in Lucas and Papanek, eds., *Indian Economy*, p. 259.

72. A. V. Desai, ed., *Technology*, esp. chap. 1, Desai's own "Technological Performance in Indian Industry"; pp. 25–27 in particular.

73. Ninan, "Business and Economy," pp. 36–37. (He does not indicate what he is measuring, whether GNP or income.)

74. Tata Services, *Statistical Outline, 1989–90*, p. 5 (table 2 for national and per capital income growth rates, and for agricultural and food-grain production figures).

75. J. C. Sandesara, "Indian Industrialisation: Tendencies, Interpretations, and Issues" (Paper prepared for the ICSSR seminar, Dec. 1988; mimeo), pp. 9–17.

76. R. Nagaraj, "Growth in Manufacturing Output Since 1980: Some Preliminary Findings," *Economic and Political Weekly* (Bombay), vol. 24, no. 26 (July 1, 1989): 1481–84. Among the critics of the base change see Kurien, "Indian Economy in the 1980's."

77. See GOI, *Economic Survey, 1989–90*, esp. chaps. 1 and 4 on the general economic situation, and on industrial performance. All the figures for fiscal year 1990–91 are preliminary estimates, and are from various late 1990 issues of *India Abroad* and the *Economic Times*.

78. Adiseshiah, *Mid-Year Review*, pp. 156–57.

79. Abid Hussain, "Indian Industry in the 1990s: Challenges Ahead," *Mainstream* (Delhi), Jan. 28, 1989, p. 41.

80. Adiseshiah, *Mid-Year Review*.

81. Hussain, "Indian Industry"; Echeverri-Gent, "Growth Performance," pp. 121–22; Tata Services, *Statistical Outline, 1989–90*, pp. 131–34 (tables 138–141), and 82 (table 80) for small-scale industry employment.

82. Ninan, "Business and Economy," p. 51.

83. Tata Services, *Statistical Outline, 1989–90*, p. 123 (tables 125 and 126).

84. Ninan, "Business and Economy," p. 59.

85. Rao, "India since Independence," p. 16.

86. Ibid., p. 17.

87. Ibid.

88. GOI, *Economic Survey, 1988–89*, pp. S-61 and S-49; Tata Services, *Statistical Outline, 1989–90*, pp. 189 (table 192) and 140 (table 150).

89. Reserve Bank of India, *Report of the Committee to Review the Working of the Monetary System* (Chakravarty Committee Report) (Bombay, 1985), pp. 17–18 for quotation.

90. GOI, *Economic Survey, 1988–89*, pp. S-36–37, and S-49; and Tata Services, *Statistical Outline, 1989–90*, pp. 140, 153–160 (tables 150, 164–173).

91. C. H. H. Rao, quoted in "Getting into Stride," *India Today*, Jan. 15, 1990, p. 36.

92. Tata Services, *Statistical Outline, 1989–90*, p. 144 (table 154) for exchange rates.

CHAPTER FIVE

1. This and many of the quotations that follow are from the very insightful contribution of Yves Chevrier, "NEP and Beyond: The Transition to 'Modernization' in China (1978–85)," in *Transforming China's Economy in the Eighties*, ed. S. Feuchtwang et al. (Boulder, 1988), vol. 1, chap. 1. I will not give specific page references to all of these quotations. Also on the differences among the Chinese leadership, see among others, H. Harding, *China's Second Revolution*, chap. 4.

2. Chevrier, "NEP and Beyond," pp. 12–13.

3. I became aware of the importance of this problem in India as a result of conversations with Phiroze Medhora.

4. I was told by Walter Hauser and Lewis P. Fickett, Jr., two distinguished political scientists who visited India during the elections or soon thereafter, that two of the leading issues on the economic side that contributed to Rajiv Gandhi's defeat were the inflation issue and the perception of corruption in the Congress. (See the article by L. Fickett, Jr., "The Janata Dal in the Ninth Indian General Election of 1989 and Its General Prospects," in H. Gould and S. Ganguly, eds., *The 1989 Elections in India* (Boulder 1991).

CHAPTER SIX

1. On the United States experience and policy response to the 1930s depression, I found P. Temins *Lessons from the Great Depression* (Cambridge, Mass., 1990) most insightful from a political economy perspective.

SELECTED
BIBLIOGRAPHY

THE following listing of books and articles makes no claim to being either all-inclusive or definitive. Rather it contains the titles referred to in the notes, together with other books that I found especially stimulating or insightful in helping me to better understand the economic reform processes of the 1980s in China and India. I have deliberately restricted the listing in this bibliography to books and articles that appeared in the 1980s and 1990s. This has inevitably excluded very important material by authors whose work I admire. But if I had included earlier material the length of the bibliography would have exceeded that of the text.

BOOKS

India, and General China
Dernberger, R. F., and Eckaus, R. S. *Financing Asian Development.* Vol. 2, *China and India.* Lanham, MD, 1988.
Feinberg, R. E., et al. *Economic Reform in Three Giants.* New Brunswick, NJ, 1990.
Indian Council of Social Science Research. *Economic Development of India and China.* New Delhi, 1988.
Perkins, D. H., and Roemer, M., eds. *Reforming Economic Systems in Developing Countries.* Cambridge, MA, 1991.
Pye, L. *Asian Power and Politics.* Cambridge, MA, 1985.
Swamy, S. *Economic Growth in China and India.* New Delhi, 1989.
Taylor, J. *The Dragon and the Wild Goose.* Westport, 1987.
Temin, P. *Lessons from The Great Depression.* Cambridge, MA, 1990.
World Bank. *World Development Report, 1991: The Challenge of Development.* New York, 1991.

China

Barnett, A. D., and Clough, R. N., eds. *Modernizing China*. Boulder, CO, 1986.

Beijing Review, China Today, (3): Economic Readjustment and Reform. Beijing, 1982.

Byrd, W. A. *The Shenyang Smelter*. Word Bank Staff Working Paper 776. Washington, DC, 1985.

Byrd, W. A., and Lin, Q., eds. *China's Rural Industry*. Washington, DC, 1990.

China, People's Republic of. State Statistical Bureau. *China Statistical Abstract, 1989*. Edited by W. T. Liu. New York, 1989.

————. *State Statistical Abstract, 1986*. Hong Kong, 1986.

Chow, G. E. *The Chinese Economy*. Cambridge, MA, 1985.

Deng, X. *Fundamental Issues in Present-Day China*. Oxford, 1987.

Dirlik, A., and Meisner, M., eds. *Marxism and the Chinese Experience*. Armonk, NY, 1989.

Duara, P. *Culture, Power and the State*. Stanford, 1989.

East-West Center, Asia—Pacific Report. Part 2, *Focus: China in the Reform Era*. Honolulu, 1989.

Fairbank, J. K. *The Great Chinese Revolution, 1800–1985*. New York, 1986.

Feuchtwang, S., et al., eds. *Transforming China's Economy in the Eighties*, vols. 1 and 2. Boulder, 1988. (Vol. 1 contains the Chevrier article "NEP and Beyond.")

Gargan, Edward G. *China's Fate*. New York, 1990.

Goodman, D. S. G., ed. *China's Regional Development*. London, 1989.

Granick, D. *Chinese State Enterprises: A Regional Property Rights Analysis*. Chicago, 1990.

Griffin, K., ed. *Institutional Reform and Economic Development in the Chinese Countryside*. London, 1984.

Harding, H. *China's Second Revolution: Reform after Mao*. Washington, DC, 1987.

Hsu, J. C. *China's Foreign Trade Reforms*. Cambridge, 1989.

Isaacs, H. *Re-Encounters in China*. Armonk, NY, 1985.

Johnson, D. G. *The People's Republic of China, 1978–1990*. San Francisco, 1991.

Kane, A. J., ed. *China Briefing, 1989*. Boulder, CO, 1989.

Kellogg, D. *In Search of China*. London, 1989.

Laaksonen, O. *Management in China during and after Mao in Enterprises, Government, and Party*. New York, 1988.

Leys, S. *The Burning Forest*. New York, 1986.

Lieberthal, K., and Oksenberg, M. *Policy Making in China*. Princeton, 1989.

Liu, B. *Tell the World*. New York, 1989.

Lyons, T. P. *Economic Integration and Planning in Maoist China* New York, 1987.

Ma Hong. *New Strategy for China's Economy*. Beijing, 1983.

Mitra, A., ed. *China: Issues in Development*. New Delhi, 1988.

Nathan, A. J. *Chinese Democracy*. London, 1986.

Nolan, P., and Dong, F., eds. *Market Forces in China*. London, 1990.

Perry, E., and Wong, C., eds. *The Political Economy of Reform in Post-Mao China*. Cambridge, MA, 1985.

Prybla, J. *The Chinese Economy*. 2d ed. Columbia, SC, 1981.

Riskin, C. *China's Political Economy*. Oxford, 1987.

Shue, V. *The Reach of the State*. Stanford, 1988.

Solinger, D. J. *China's Business under Socialism*. Berkley, 1987.

Spence, J. *The Search for Modern China*. New York, 1990.

Tidrick, G., and Jiyuan, C., eds. *China's Industrial Reform*. Washington, DC, 1987.

Tsou, T. *The Cultural Revolution and Post-Mao Reforms*. Chicago, 1986.

U.S. Congress. Joint Economic Committee. *China's Economy Looks toward the Year 2000*. Washington, DC, 1986.

Vogel, E. *One Step Ahead in China*. Cambridge, MA, 1989.

Walder, A. *Communist Neo-Traditionalism*. Berkley, 1986.

Wang, G. C., ed. *Economic Reform in the PRC*. Boulder, CO, 1982.

White, L. III. *Policies of Chaos*. Princeton, 1989.

Woodruff, J. *China in Search of Its Future*. Seattle, 1989.

World Bank. *China: Finance and Investment*. Washington, DC, 1988.

Xue, M. *China's Socialist Economy*. Beijing, 1980.

India

Adiseshiah, M. S. *Mid-Year Review of the Indian Economy: 1987–88*. New Delhi, 1988.

Ahluwalia, I. J. *Industrial Growth in India*. Delhi, 1985.

Bardhan, P. K. *The Political Economy of Development in India*. Oxford, 1984.

Bouton, M., and Oldenburg, P., eds. *India Briefing, 1989* and *India Briefing, 1990*. Boulder, CO, 1989 and 1990.

Brahmananda, P. R., and Panchamuklu, V. R. *The Development Process of the Indian Economy*. Bombay, 1987.

Centre for Monitoring the Indian Economy (CMIE). *The Liberalization Process*. Bombay, 1986.

——. *Production and Capacity Utilization in 600 Industries 1970–1986*. Bombay, 1987.

Chakravarty, S. *Development Planning: The Indian Experience*. Oxford, 1988.

Dasgupta, A., and Sengupta, N. K. *Government and Business.* New Delhi, 1988.

Desai, A. V., ed. *Technology Absorption in Indian Industry.* New Delhi, 1988.

India, Government of (GOI). Ministry of Finance. *Economic Surveys, 1984–85; 1987–88; 1988–89; and 1989–90.* New Delhi, 1985, 1988, 1989, and 1990.

———. Planning Commission. *The Seventh Five Year Plan, 1985–90.* New Delhi, 1985.

International Labor Organization (ILO-ARTEP). *Employment and Structural Change in Indian Industries.* Geneva, 1989.

Jannuzi, F. T. *India in Transition.* Boulder, CO, 1989.

Jha, L. K. *Mr. Red Tape.* New Delhi, 1987.

Kohli, A. *The State and Poverty in India.* Cambridge, 1987.

Little, I. M. D., et al. *Small Manufacturing Enterprises: . . . India and Other Economies.* Oxford, 1987.

Lucas, R. E. B., and Papanek, G., eds. *The Indian Economy.* Boulder, CO, 1988.

Marathe, S. S. *Regulation and Development.* New Delhi, 1986.

Naipaul, V. S. *India: A Million Mutinies Now.* New York, 1990.

Oldenburg, P., ed. *India Briefing, 1991.* Boulder, CO, 1991.

Pendse, D. R. *Black Money and Budgets.* New Delhi, 1984.

Pulley, R. *Making the Poor Creditworthy.* World Bank Working Paper. Washington, DC, 1989.

Ranade, S. *Competitive Democracies: The Case of Targeted Transfers in India.* Ph.D. thesis, Princeton University, 1991.

Rao, V. K. R. V. *India's National Income: 1950–1980.* New Delhi, 1983.

Reserve Bank of India. *Report of the Committee to Review the Working of the Monetary System.* Bombay, 1985.

Rosen, G. *Industrial Change in India, 1970–2000.* Riverdale, MD, 1988.

Rudolph, L., and Rudolph, S. *In Pursuit of Lakshmi.* Chicago, 1988.

Sandesara, J. C. *Efficacy of Incentives for Small Industries.* Bombay, 1982.

Sankar, T. L., and Reddy, Y. V., eds. *Privatization.* Hyderabad, 1989.

Sau, R. *India's Economic Development.* New Delhi, 1981.

Sundrum, R. M. *Growth and Income Distribution in India.* New Delhi, 1987.

Tata Services. *Statistical Outline of India, 1986–87; 1987; 1988–89; 1989–90,* ed. D. R. Pendse. Bombay, 1986, 1987, 1988, 1989.

Thomas, R. *India's Emergence as an Industrial Power.* New Delhi, 1982.

Weiner, M. *The Child and the State in India.* Princeton, 1991.

Wolf, M. *India's Exports*. Washington, DC, 1982.

World Bank. *India: An Industrializing Economy in Transition*. Washington, DC, 1989.

ARTICLES

India, and General China

Lefeber, L. "The Socialist Experience in Greece." *International Journal of Political Economy*, vol. 19, no. 4.

Malenbaum, W. "A Gloomy Portrait of Development Achievements and Prospects: China and India." *Economic Development and Cultural Change*, vol. 38, no. 2.

Nafziger, W. "India versus China: Economic Development Performance." *Dalhousie Review*, vol. 65, no. 3.

Rosen, G. "India and China: Perspectives on . . . Economic Reform." *Journal of Asian Economics*, vol. 1, no. 2.

Sen, A. "Development: Which Way Now?" *Economic Journal*, vol. 93.

———. "Food and Freedom." Sir John Crawford Memorial Lecture, Washington, DC, Oct. 1987.

Srinivasan, T. N. "External Sector and Development: China and India, 1950–89." *American Economic Review*, vol. 80, no. 2.

China

Chen, K. et al. together with G. H. Jefferson and T. G. Rawski, "Productivity Change in Chinese Industry: 1953–85," *Journal of Comparative Economics*, vol. 12 (1988).

Chen, Y., et al. "Reform: Results and Lessons from the 1985 CESRRI Survey." *Journal of Comparative Economics*, vol. 11 (1987).

Chien, C. C. "The Recent Inflation in the People's Republic of China." Paper delivered at the Conference on U.S.-Asia Economic Relations, New York, June 18–22, 1989. Mimeo.

Cohen, P. A. "The Post-Mao Reforms in Historical Perspective." *Journal of Asian Studies*, vol. 47, no. 3 (Aug. 1988).

Dernberger, R. F. "Reforms in China: Implications for U.S. Policy." *American Economic Review*, vol. 79, no. 2.

Dittmer, L. "China in 1988." *Asian Survey*, vol. 29, no. 1 (Jan. 1989).

Dong, Fureng. "'Losing Shape' in Course of Reform." FBIS-CHI-88-251, Dec. 30, 1988.

Findlay, C., Mayer, P., and Watson, A. "Fighting for the Fleece." Mimeo, Sept. 1989.

Hussain, Athar. "Chinese Economic Reforms: Irregularities and Crimes." Paper presented at Harvard University, May 1988. Mimeo.

———. "Enterprise Reform in China." Paper presented in Beijing, April 1989. Mimeo.

Ishimura, K. "China's Multiple Price System." *Japan External Trade Organization: China Newsletter*, no. 80 (May–June 1989).

Lardy, N. "Sustaining Development." Paper presented at the Woodrow Wilson International Center, 1991, and summarized in the *Woodrow Wilson Center Report*, vol. 2, no. 5 (March 1991): 1–2.

Lin, C. C. "China's Economic Reforms II: Western Perspectives." *Asian-Pacific Economic Literature*, vol. 2, no. 1.

———. "The Reinstatement of Economics in China Today." *China Quarterly* (March 1981).

Lin, Z. "The Price Situation." *Beijing Review, China Today (3)* (1982), appendix, pp. 203–7.

Little, D. "Development Traps in Traditional and Modern China." Paper presented at the Association for Asian Studies meetings, 1990. Mimeo.

Luo, Y. "Structural Reform and Economic Development in China." *International Social Science Journal*, no. 120 (May 1989).

Manohoran, T. "Current Rural Organizational Structure in the PRC." Mimeo; LSE-ICRIER Seminar on Large Economies: China and India. January 1990.

Myers, R. H. "How Can We Evaluate Communist China's Economic Development Performance?" *Issues and Studies*, vol. 23, no. 2.

———. "Mainland China's March toward a New Socialism." Pp. 63–74 in *Thinking about America: The U.S. in the 1990's*. Stanford, 1988.

Naughton, B. "The Third Front: Defence Industrialization in the Chinese Interior." *China Quarterly*, no. 115 (Sept. 1988).

Oi, J. C. "Economic Management and Rural Government." Paper read at the 1990 meeting of the Association for Asian Studies. Mimeo.

Pann, L. "The New Chinese Revolution." *Antioch Review*, vol. 46, no. 2.

Perkins, D. "Reforming China's Economic System." *Journal of Economic Literature*, vol. 26, no. 2 (June 1988).

Prime, P. "Central-Provincial Investment and Finance: The Cultural Revolution . . . in Jiangsu Province." Chap. 9 in *New Perspectives on the Cultural Revolution*, ed. W. S. Joseph et al. Cambridge, MA, 1991.

Prybyla, J. S. "China's Economic Experiment: Back from the Market?" *Problems of Communism* (Jan.–Feb. 1989).

Qimiao, F. "Compendium of Literature on Price and Price Reform in China." London School of Economics, China Programme, *Research into . . . Pricing . . . in China*, paper no. 2 (May 1989).

Reynolds, B. "The Chinese Economy in 1988." Asia Society, *China Briefing* (1989).

Solinger, D. J. "Capitalist Measures with Chinese Characteristics." *Problems of Communism* (Jan.–Feb. 1989).

———. "Economic Reform in China." *Harvard International Review,* vol. 11, no. 2.

Sung, Y. W., and Chan, T. M. H. "China's Economic Reforms I: The Debates in China." *Asian-Pacific Economic Literature,* vol. 1, no. 1 (May 1987).

Taylor, R. "Chinese Hierarchy in Comparative Perspective." *Journal of Asian Studies,* vol. 48, no. 3 (Aug. 1989).

Walder, A. G. "Wage Reform and the Web of Factory Interests." *China Quarterly,* no. 109 (March 1987).

Wang, J. "Geographic Concentration and Export Instability: A Case Study of China." Mimeo, 1990.

Wong, C. P. "Between Plan and Market: The Role of the Local Sector in Post-Mao China." *Journal of Comparative Economics,* vol. 11 (1987).

Wu, J., and Reynolds, B. "Choosing a Strategy for China's Economic Reform." *American Economic Review,* vol. 78, no. 2.

Zhang, Z. "The Chinese Economic Regulatory Mechanism in Transformation." *Journal of Asian Economics,* vol. 1, no. 1.

Zhao, L. "Thinking of Reform of the Chinese Fiscal and Financial System to Deal with Inflation." Unpublished paper, 1991.

Zhao, Z. "Advance along the Road of Socialism with Chinese Characteristics." *Documents of the Thirteenth National Congress of the Communist Party of China.* Beijing, 1987.

Journals (Entire Issues)

Beijing Review, vol. 27, no. 44, supplement, Oct. 29, 1984. "Decision of the Central Committee of the Communist Party of China on Reform of the Economic Structure."

Copenhagen Papers in East and Southeast Asian Studies (Jan. 1987). K. Brodsgaard, ed., "Ten Years After: Economic and Political Reform in Post-Mao China."

Economist, vol. 304, no. 7509 (August 1, 1987). "China's Economy: A Survey."

Journal of Asian Economics, vol. 1, no. 2 (Fall 1990). "Perspectives on Recent Economic Developments in China: A Symposium"; as well as other articles on China, outside the symposium. Also vol. 2, no. 2 (Fall 1991), with four articles on Chinese economic reform.

Journal of International Affairs (Columbia University), vol. 39, no. 2 (Winter 1986). "China in Transition."

New York Times, 1989–91. Articles by N. Kristof and S. WuDunn.

Woodrow Wilson Center Report, vol. 2, no. 5 (March 1991). Summaries of papers by N. Lardy and B. Liu, on China's recent economic and political changes.

See also numerous articles in the *Beijing Review* and the *Far Eastern Economic Review,* 1986–90; the *Asian-Pacific Economic Literature,* in its five volumes from 1987 to 1991 has published numerous scholarly articles and reviews of economic issues in China.

India

Adams, J. "Breaking Away: India's Economy Vaults into the 1990's." Asia Society, *India Briefing 1990.*

Desai, N. "Development Planning in Review." Paper for the Indian Council for Social Science Research conferences, Dec. 1988. Mimeo.

Dhar, P. N. "India since Independence." *Times of India* (Bombay), Dec. 12–16, 1988.

———. "The Political Economy of Development in India." *Indian Economic Review,* vol. 22, no. 1 (Jan.–June 1987).

Fickett, L. P., Jr. "The Janata Dal in the Ninth Indian General Election of 1989 and Its Future Prospects." In H. Gould and S. Ganguly, eds., *The 1989 Elections in India.* Boulder, 1991.

Hussain, Abid. "Indian Industry in the 1990s: Challenges Ahead." *Mainstream* (Delhi), Jan. 28, 1989.

Joseph, K. J. "Growth Performance of Indian Electronics under Liberalization." *Economic and Political Weekly* (Bombay), vol. 24 (Aug. 19, 1989).

Kochanek, S. A. "Briefcase Politics in India: The Congress Party and the Business Elite." *Asian Survey,* vol. 27, no. 12 (Dec. 1987).

Kohli, A. "Politics of Economic Liberalization in India." *World Development,* vol. 17, no. 3.

Krishnaswamy, K. S. "What Ails the Public Sector?" Agit Bhagat Memorial Lecture, Ahmedabad, 1980.

Kurien, C. T. "Indian Economy in the 1980s and on to the 1990s." *Bulletin of the Madras Institute of Development Studies,* vol. 19, no. 1 (Jan. 1989).

———. "Planning and Institutional Transformation of the Indian Economy." *Social Scientist,* vol. 15, no. 7 (1987).

Meyer, R. C. "How Do Indians Vote?" *Asian Survey,* vol. 29, no. 12 (Dec. 1989): 1111–22.

Mukhopadhyay, J. K. "Estimates of Poverty Statistics in India: A Close Look." *Journal of Income and Wealth* (Bombay), vol. 10, no. 1 (Jan. 1988).

Nagaraj, R. "Growth in Manufacturing Output Since 1980." *Economic and Political Weekly,* vol. 24, no. 26.

————. "Industrial Growth: Further Evidence. . . ." *Economic and Political Weekly,* 25, no. 41.

Ninan, T. N. "Business and Economy: Reaching Out and Upward." Asia Society, *India Briefing 1989.*

Patel, I. G. "On Taking India into the Twenty First Century: New Economic Policy in India." *Modern Asian Studies,* vol. 21, no. 2 (1987).

Pendse, D. R. "The Message of the Seventh Five Year Plan." Inaugural Lecture, Dr. Helekar Memorial Lecture Series, Goa, Feb. 7, 1986.

Raj, K. N. "New Economic Policy." V. T. Krishnamachari Lecture, Delhi, 1985.

Rao, V. K. R. V. "India since Independence." *Mainstream,* Jan. 28, 1989.

Riedel, J. et al. "Determinants of Indian Export Performance in the 1970s." *Weltwirtschaftliches Archiv,* vol. 120, no. 1 (1984).

Sandesara, J. C. "Indian Industrialization: Tendencies, Interpretations, and Issues." Paper for the Indian Council for Social Research conference, Dec. 1988. Mimeo.

————. "Public Sector in India." University of Baroda, D. K. Shukla Memorial Lecture, Feb. 23, 1991. Mimeo.

Vaidyanathan, A. "State and Economic Development in India." *Bulletin of the Madras Institute of Development Studies,* vol. 19, no. 1 (Jan. 1989).

Journals

Economic and Political Weekly (Bombay), 1985–91. Numerous important articles on Indian economic and political issues.

Economic Times (Bombay). A daily paper on economic events in India.

India Abroad. A weekly newspaper for the Indian overseas community, published in the United States, with articles on current events in India.

India Today. A biweekly Indian journal of current events.

Journal of Comparative Economics, vol. 14. no. 4 (Dec. 1990) contains three interesting articles on planning in India, and one on planning in China.

Journal of the Indian School of Political Economy (Pune, India). This is a new journal that first appeared in 1989. It has some of the most interesting articles currently being published on Indian political economy.

Seminar (New Delhi), 1988–90 issues. A monthly journal, each issue devoted to a particular aspect of Indian society.

INDEX

Accumulation, share of, relative to consumption, China, 41, 56, 90–91
Administrative system. *See* Bureaucracy
Agricultural reform
—China, 77, 85, 89, 90, 113–14, 119, 128; freeing of marketing and price controls on farm products, 53, 61; and investment, 56; start of, 52–53, 128
—India, 107, 113, 129, 132–33, 135
Agriculture (*see also* Agricultural reform): numbers engaged in, China and India, 2
—China: commune system, 4, 48, 85; decline in exports, 93; growth of farm output, 48, 53, 89; investment in, 56, 77; lack of investment in, 3, 41, 48, 91–92
—India: and Green Revolution, 49, 77, 135; lack of investment in, 3, 49, 77, 112; land reform after independence, 6; and Integrated Rural Development Poverty Program, 30–31; power of state governments concerning, 23, 32
Ahluwalia, Montek, 68
Anhui province, China, 52, 119
Automobile industry. *See* Motor vehicle industry

Banking system (*see also* Macroeconomic regulatory system)
—China, 22, 89, 91, 115, 122; abolition of, 32; weakness of, 4; increase in lending, 87–88
—India (*see also* Reserve Bank of India): development banks, 7; nationalization of, 6, 27, 30
Bankruptcy: China, 64, 115; India, 101, 115
Barter, of industrial inputs and outputs, China, 38
Black market (*see also* Corruption): China, 121, 128; India, 49, 100
Bofors scandal in India, 75
British government in India, 25
Bureaucracy
—China, 20–21, 22, 32, 60; and Communist party, 9; and the Cultural Revolution, 14; Deng's attitude toward, 18; as force for continuity, 32; effect of reform on, 83, 121; and tendency toward central planning, 19
—India (*see also* Indian Administrative Service; Licensing system): 24–25, 27–28, 32, 45; as force for continuity, 32; and reform policies, 75, 110; relationship to Congress party, 9

Capital goods, import of (*see also* Trade): China, 93; India, 72, 111
Capital goods sector: China, 3, 37; India, 3, 25, 72, 111
Capital investment. *See* Investment

159